amnesty international
HANDBOOK

amnesty international
HANDBOOK

amnesty international
HANDBOOK

amnesty international
HANDBOOK

amnesty international
HANDBOOK

© Amnesty International Publications 1983
All rights reserved.
First edition: ''Handbook for Groups'', 1962
Second edition: ''How to help prisoners of conscience: a handbook for groups'', 1967
Third edition: ''Handbook for Groups'', March 1971
Fourth edition: ''Handbook for Groups'', March 1973
Fifth edition: March 1977
Sixth edition: February 1983
ISBN: 0 900058 48 X
Original language: English
AI Index: ORG 02/01/83
Published by Amnesty International Publications

Copies of Amnesty International Publications can be obtained from the offices of the sections of Amnesty International. Office addresses and further information may be obtained from the International Secretariat, 10 Southampton Street, London WC2E 7HF, United Kingdom. Address after September 1983: Amnesty International, International Secretariat, 1 Easton Street, London WC1, United Kingdom.

Cover design by Ian Franklin. Printed in Great Britain by Russell Press Ltd, Gamble Street, Nottingham, England.

# CONTENTS

Preface      HOW TO USE THIS HANDBOOK      1

Chapter 1      A CONSPIRACY OF HOPE      3

Chapter 2      AMNESTY INTERNATIONAL TODAY      5

Chapter 3      POLITICAL IMPRISONMENT, TORTURE AND EXECUTIONS      7
The mandate
Prisoners of conscience
Political trials
Torture
The death penalty
Political killings by governments
"Disappearances"
Prison conditions
Refugees

Chapter 4      HOW AMNESTY INTERNATIONAL WORKS      14
Research
Case work
Campaigns
Campaign for the Abolition of Torture
Program for the Abolition of the Death Penalty
Urgent Actions
Campaign for Prisoners of the Month
Prisoners of Conscience Week
Country campaigns and special actions
Regional Action Networks
Missions
Relief
Publicity and Publications
Representations to National Governments
The United Nations and International Organizations
Target Sector Work
Human Rights Education

Chapter 5      AMNESTY INTERNATIONAL THROUGHOUT THE WORLD      23
Members and subscribers
Local AI Groups
Sections
The International Council
International Executive Committee
International Committees
International Secretariat

Chapter 6      FUND-RAISING AND FINANCES      31

Chapter 7      ONE MOVEMENT, ONE VOICE      35
International team work
Speaking to the news media
Publications
An international personality

Chapter 8          GENERAL ADVICE ON ACTION                         42
                   Security
                   Coordinating activities
                   Relations with international organizations
                   Relations with other organizations
                   What is pressure?
                   Letters
                   Appeals
                   Delegations
                   Public actions
                   Symbolic actions
                   Performances
                   Target sector work

Chapter 9          CASE WORK                                        50
                   Responsibilities of an AI Group
                   International Secretariat liaison with local AI groups
                   Coordination
                   Selection of prisoner cases
                   Closure of cases
                   Aftercare
                   Correspondence with government authorities
                   Correspondence and meetings with government
                       representatives
                   Publicity and press relations
                   Approaches to other organizations and institutions
                   Correspondence with AI contacts
                   Correspondence with the prisoner and family
                   Relief
                   Visits to the prisoner's country

Chapter 10         LETTERS AND TELEGRAMS                            59

Chapter 11         AMNESTY INTERNATIONAL POLICY                     63
                   Statute of Amnesty International
                   Impartiality and the Defence of Human Rights
                   Amnesty International and the Use of Violence
                   Policy Guidelines on Conscientious Objection
                   Declaration of Stockholm
                   Guidelines for Sections and Groups
                   Guidelines on AI Sections' Activities concerning Human
                       Rights Violations in their own Countries
                   Guidelines for the Acceptance of Financial Contributions
                       and Fund-raising by AI

Chapter 12         HUMAN RIGHTS IN INTERNATIONAL LAW                83

Chapter 13         WORKING RULES                                    89
                   Publicity and publications
                   Statements on members' countries
                   External relations
                   Case work and campaigns
                   Missions/AI travel
                   International cooperation
                   Finance, fund-raising and relief
                   Membership, internal structures and information
                       handling

Chapter 14         COMMONLY ASKED QUESTIONS                         94

                   INDEX                                            96

# How to use this Handbook

This is the sixth edition of the *Amnesty International Handbook*. It is a basic reference manual for Amnesty International (AI) members, particularly those working in local groups. It has been prepared by the movement's International Secretariat and is available in various languages and local editions. Copies can be obtained from the International Secretariat or from section offices.

New AI members should not feel obliged to read and immediately digest all the information it contains. However, members are expected to be familiar with the policies and rules explained in it. There is a list of chapter headings at the beginning and an index at the end: these indicate the information contained in the handbook.

The material is presented in three parts:

*First Part.* The first six chapters introduce AI's worldwide activities and structure. The last chapter, "Commonly Asked Questions", gives concise answers to questions members often face.

*Second Part.* Chapters 7, 8, 9 and 10 give suggestions for group work and campaigns. Groups should consult the handbook before undertaking activities. Note that these chapters give only general advice. Groups working on individual cases receive prisoner dossiers with detailed instructions: these *take precedence at all times* over these general suggestions.

*Third Part.* Chapters 11, 12 and 13 include reference material on AI policy and human rights in international law. The *Working Rules* in Chapter 13 specify the *responsibilities* of all parts of the movement and the normal procedures of the organization.

New working methods are always being developed. This diversity and flexibility is one of the strengths of the movement. As a result the handbook can never be a definitive document. To check up on any current policy or to obtain advice on particular problems, please consult your coordination group, section office or the International Secretariat.

# Chapter 1

# A conspiracy of hope

Amnesty International was launched in 1961 to bring out of the dungeons the forgotten prisoners. It began with a newspaper article calling on people of all walks of life to begin working impartially and peacefully for the release of thousands of men and women imprisoned throughout the world for their political and religious beliefs. These were to be called "prisoners of conscience", and with that a new phrase entered the vocabulary of world affairs.

Within a month more than a thousand people had sent in offers of practical help. Six months later founder Peter Benenson announced a further step in the campaign. What had started as a brief publicity effort was being converted into a permanent international movement.

"We believe that these first six months have shown that in an increasingly cynical world there is a great latent reservoir of idealism to be tapped," he declared.

The full capacity of that reservoir would be needed if practical action were to counter the reality of political persecution. Trade unionists were being arrested in Spain, dissenters faced long prison terms in the German Democratic Republic, detainees in South Africa were subjected to brutality and ill-treatment in custody, civil rights workers in the United States of America were being persecuted, political trials were taking place in the Soviet Union.

## Official silence

In each case where the free expression of views was being suppressed by torture and imprisonment, Amnesty International members (slowly being organized into groups) attempted the seemingly impossible. They began their own battle against official silence and political persecution. They contacted the prisoners' families and lawyers and began sending off postcards, letters and telegrams appealing to government authorities to respect human rights.

An early supporter of the movement, the humanitarian Dr Albert Schweitzer, underlined the significance of Amnesty International's purpose. In a special message in 1963, he wrote: "I believe that world peace can only be achieved when there is freedom for people of all politics, religions and races to exchange their views in a continuing dialogue. For this reason I would particularly ask all those who are working in their different ways towards world peace to make their contribution, preferably by active service or, failing that, by financial contribution, to this great new endeavour called Amnesty International."

Not everyone was of that view. As the move-

**Pablo Picasso was an early supporter of the Amnesty International movement, to which he gave this drawing.**

ment became better known and attracted more support, its critics became vocal. A report on allegations of ill-treatment of detainees in

Northern Ireland caused a furore in the United Kingdom, the country where the Amnesty appeal had first appeared. As other reports came out on country after country, denunciations followed. The Soviet journal *Izvestia* referred to "ideological saboteurs"; *Rastakhiz* in Iran dubbed Amnesty "a new puppet show that the communists have started".

But from inside the very countries that were damning Amnesty came other voices. The postcards and the telegrams and the little parcels of medicine were getting through. Letters came back, many of them smuggled out of prison or past airport censors. "We have been able to face our problems with great determination as a result of encouragement from people like you," wrote Winnie Mandela, one of the best-known leaders of Black opinion in South Africa. "We know that we are not alone in our lifelong battle. We owe this feeling to you. . . ."

From the labour camps, from the torture cells, from the families and lawyers came new accounts of torture, of psychiatric abuse, of secret executions. And always the insistent appeal: "You must do whatever you can to help us."

Faced with mounting evidence of the atrocities being inflicted on prisoners, an epidemic that seemed to spread like a cancer in the seventies, Amnesty International launched a global campaign for the abolition of torture. The voice of the movement took on a new determination.

Wherever prisoners were being subjected to torture — there were dozens of nations where the practice had become systematic, leading to mutilation and deaths in detention — Amnesty International would intervene. A new network was set up, using telephones, post office boxes, telegrams and telex machines to alert volunteers if torture was a possibility. Once a report was checked, hundreds of appeals could be on their way within hours. It became a life saving operation.

## Ordeal of torture

Among the many victims was a teacher. While he was being tortured by the police they opened a telephone line between the torture chamber and the prisoner's home, forcing his wife to listen to her husband's screams. During that ordeal she died of a heart attack. The prisoner himself survived and was eventually allowed to go into exile with his children. He told us: "They killed my wife. They would have killed me too; but you intervened and saved my life."

Another voice from prison: "Faith in your efforts and concern sustained me throughout the horrible period of my imprisonment. Without hope I think I would have died."

The movement had become a lifeline — a "conspiracy of hope", open to everyone prepared to work in defence of human dignity. It had proved that ordinary people could work together regardless of politics in an effort to halt the excesses of tyranny.

The award of the Nobel Peace Prize in 1977 brought with it a reaffirmation of the original Amnesty vision. In making the award, the Nobel Committee stated: "The world has witnessed an increasing brutalization, and internationalization of violence, terrorism and torture. . . . Through its activity for the defence of human worth against degrading treatment, violence and torture, Amnesty International has contributed to securing the ground for freedom, for justice, and thereby also for peace in the world."

We in Amnesty International are less confident. Countless prisoners remain. Torture remains. Executions are reported daily. Now human rights run the risk of being dragged down in the tangle of international power politics.

## Complete independence

Faced with this challenge, our complete independence is even more imperative. We have an obligation to keep partisan politics out of the work for prisoners of conscience. We have an obligation to maintain the highest possible standards of accuracy in our reports. We have to keep Amnesty International true to its own ideal — an independent people's movement defending the victims of political imprisonment, torture and the death sentence.

We need every donation anyone can send us. But we need more. We need commitment. We need people prepared to work for the release of prisoners of conscience and to send telegrams or write letters or stand in the rain outside embassies or do whatever has to be done to stop the next wave of torture and executions.

This is a long-standing commitment we have made to the prisoners. As long as they are incarcerated for their beliefs we must be ready to use our freedom in defence of theirs.

This statement was issued for the 20th anniversary of Amnesty International in 1981.

# Chapter 2

# Amnesty International Today

Thousands of people are in prison because of their beliefs. Many are held without charge or trial. Torture and the death penalty are widespread. In many countries, men, women and children have "disappeared" after being taken into official custody. Others have been put to death without any pretence of legality: selected and killed by governments and their agents.

Despite efforts at the United Nations and in the field of international law, the world still lacks efficient machinery to prevent these and other violations of human rights. Perhaps the only alternative which has proved at all effective has been the force of aroused world opinion. This is the fundamental belief and experience upon which the work of Amnesty International (AI) is based.

AI plays a specific role in the international protection of human rights. Its activities focus on prisoners:

● It seeks the *release* of men and women detained anywhere for their beliefs, colour, sex, ethnic origin, language or religion, provided they have not used or advocated violence. These are *"prisoners of conscience"*.

● It advocates *fair and prompt trials* for *all political prisoners* and works on behalf of such people detained without charge or without trial.

● It opposes the death penalty and torture or other cruel, inhuman or degrading treatment or punishment of *all prisoners* without reservation.

AI does not support or oppose any government or political system. Its members around the world include supporters of differing systems who agree on the need to protect all people in all countries from imprisonment for their beliefs, and from torture and execution.

Today, AI has more than 350,000 members, subscribers and supporters in over 150 countries and territories with organized sections in more than 40 of them. Its International Secretariat in London has a staff of about 150. Each year the movement handles, on average, nearly 5,000 individual cases regardless of the ideology of either the victims or the governments concerned.

The advantage of AI's approach is that it promotes respect for universal principles not only at the level of governments and international organizations but also through the concerted action of individuals working in small local groups.

Whenever AI hears of political arrests or of people threatened with torture or execution it concentrates first on getting the facts. At the International Secretariat researchers collect and check every available detail in order to build up profiles of the prisoners and the circumstances under which they have been detained. The Research Department receives information from many sources including hundreds of newspapers and journals, government bulletins, transcripts of radio broadcasts, reports from lawyers and human rights organizations, as well as letters from prisoners and their families. AI also sends fact-finding missions for on-the-spot investigations and to observe trials, meet prisoners and interview government officials.

When the facts have been established, efforts on behalf of the prisoners can get underway. The local groups and sections then undertake the vital work of demonstrating international concern for the protection of the basic human rights violated in each case. Government and prison officials are faced with insistent, continuous and informed appeals. Letter after letter goes to cabinet ministers and embassies. AI members try to get publicity in their local press. Influential people are asked to sign petitions and support protests.

A unique aspect of the case work — placing the emphasis on the need for international protection of human rights — is the fact that each group works on behalf of prisoners held in countries other than its own. The working methods of the movement reflect this principle and ensure that impartiality and independence remain fundamental to all AI's activities. No members are expected to provide information on their own countries and no members have responsibility for action taken or statements issued by AI about their own countries.

If it is clear that the victims are prisoners of conscience, their cases are allocated for adoption to one or more local groups. Group members study the background to each case and organize appeals for the prisoner's immediate and unconditional release. Every group is assigned responsibility for at least two prisoner cases, balanced geographically and politically to reflect the movement's impartiality.

In addition to working for the release of prisoners of conscience, AI tries to give them and their families humanitarian assistance during the period of detention. Funds are raised for food, clothing and schooling; books are supplied for students whose arrest interrupts their education. Occasionally assistance is provided for legal aid.

When mass political arrests take place, it may sometimes be impossible to identify each of the victims. The scale of the arrests and the procedures to keep the detainees in custody may make it difficult to establish whether they are prisoners of conscience. But wherever people are being held on politically related grounds AI groups urge the government concerned to give them fair and prompt trials or release them.

In many cases individual prisoners are released after sustained efforts by AI groups. Some are freed soon after their cases are taken up; some are released in general amnesties; others serve their entire sentences before gaining their freedom. AI does not claim credit for the release of any prisoner. But once a case is taken up for adoption, AI never gives up its efforts.

As well as seeking the release of prisoners of conscience and fair and prompt trials in political cases, AI campaigns for the abolition of torture and the death penalty in all cases. This includes trying to prevent torture and executions when

people have been taken to known torture centres or have been sentenced to death. Volunteers in dozens of countries can be alerted in such cases, and within hours hundreds of telegrams and other appeals can be on their way to the government, prison or detention centre.

AI group members also take part in national and international publicity drives to draw attention to patterns of human rights abuses in various countries. These often highlight practices such as widespread detention without trial; laws used to imprison people for the non-violent exercise of their rights; the systematic use of torture; political killings and executions.

The symbol of Amnesty International is a lighted candle surrounded by barbed wire.

To monitor the observance of international legal standards in political cases and to make representations on behalf of prisoners AI undertakes a number of missions each year. On the basis of these missions and its research activities AI issues statements to the world press and publishes major reports.

AI is financed by its worldwide membership, by individual subscriptions and by donations. Members pay membership fees (varying from country to country) and conduct fund-raising campaigns in their local communities. Strict guidelines for the acceptance of funds stipulate that any "funds requested and accepted by Amnesty International must in no way incur financial dependence, real or apparent, upon any political interest or group singly or in combination, nor limit the freedom of activity and expression enjoyed by the organization, nor direct its areas of concern". The accounts are audited annually and are published with the organization's annual report.

AI has formal relations with the United Nations, UNESCO, and the Council of Europe, the Organization of American States and the Organization of African Unity. In 1977 it was awarded the Nobel Peace Prize and in 1978 the United Nations Human Rights Prize.

# Chapter 3

# Political Imprisonment, Torture and Executions

## The mandate

At the core of AI's work is its "mandate" which determines the scope and limitations of its activity. The mandate applies to three different, but overlapping, categories of prisoner: *all* prisoners, *political* prisoners and *prisoners of conscience*. It specifies what AI may do on behalf of prisoners in each of these categories. This can be represented, for the purpose of demonstration, by using the flame of the lighted AI candle.

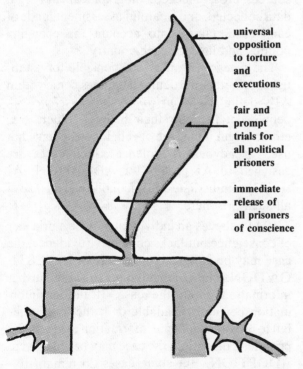

universal opposition to torture and executions

fair and prompt trials for all political prisoners

immediate release of all prisoners of conscience

In the case of *all* prisoners, AI opposes the death penalty and torture or other cruel, inhuman or degrading treatment or punishment. This category can be seen as the all-embracing, outer edge of the flame. Within that, as we move towards the centre of the flame, is the category of all *political* prisoners. Wherever such prisoners are held AI works to ensure that they have fair and prompt trials. Moving again to the centre of the flame, we come to the category of *prisoners of conscience* — people detained because of their beliefs, colour, sex, ethnic origin, language or religion who have not used or advocated violence. Their imprisonment is, in itself, a violation of the Universal Declaration of Human Rights and AI works for their immediate and unconditional release.

These essential elements of the mandate are set forth in the first article of the AI Statute, which is reproduced in full in Chapter 11. It can be amended only by a two-thirds vote of all delegates attending a meeting of the International Council, the movement's supreme governing body.

As patterns of human rights abuses vary and as AI becomes more deeply involved in combating them, there are often precise points on which the mandate needs clarification. Such issues are referred to the International Council for decision after study and debate. If AI members want further information on mandate issues not dealt with in this handbook, they should consult their coordination group or section.

## Prisoners of conscience

It is impossible to calculate how many prisoners of conscience are held throughout the world. In many countries secrecy and censorship hinder the flow of information about such people to the outside world. What is certain is that for each name that is known there are many more that are unknown.

Some names are known in the outside world — leaders of political parties or trade unions, or those who have forcefully and outspokenly dissented from official views. But these are the famous few. The majority are ordinary men and women who are detained for the non-violent exercise of their rights.

Many prisoners of conscience are held for trying to exercise their inalienable rights to freedom of expression, association, assembly or movement. Many have dissented individually from government policy. Some are detained because they belong to political or religious associations. Some are conscientious objectors to military service. Others are imprisoned simply because members of their families are political or religious activists. Some have themselves tried to publicize human rights violations in their countries.

Prisoners of conscience can be held anywhere—in jails, barracks, remote islands or camps such as the one seen in this clandestine photo.

Members of national minorities in a number of countries have been jailed for trying to achieve some degree of autonomy. Trade union activity or participation in strikes or demonstrations is a common cause of imprisonment. In certain countries members of religious groups are arrested for religious practices prescribed by their faith which exceed the limits set by the state for religious activity.

Few states openly admit that they have detained people in violation of international standards. Many governments refer to a threat to national security and apply legislation which defines the threat so broadly that anyone believed to be critical of official policies can be locked away. Common to most government responses is an effort to obscure or withhold the

facts, usually from both local and world opinion.

Imprisonment takes different forms. Most prisoners of conscience are held in prisons, camps, interrogation centres or army barracks. Many others are held under house arrest, physically restricted by "banning" orders or sent into internal exile in remote places. Some have been forcibly confined to psychiatric hospitals. Each case needs rigorous and painstaking assessment. Information reaches the Research Department of the International Secretariat in many ways. It comes from the world press, which is scanned both at the International Secretariat and in the section offices; from prisoners and their families, often sent at great personal risk; from lawyers, refugees and religious bodies; from national and international organizations; and from AI's own missions to countries. All this mass of information is carefully examined, sources cross-checked, biographical and legal data collected, and a careful assessment made of each case, taking into account the changing politics and laws of each country.

The research staff are responsible for establishing whether particular detainees come within AI's definition of *prisoners of conscience* — people detained for their beliefs, colour, sex, ethnic origin, language or religion, who have not used or advocated violence. Such cases are assigned to AI groups for ADOPTION: AI seeks the immediate and unconditional release of all such prisoners.

If AI believes an individual may be a prisoner of conscience but lacks conclusive evidence, the case may be assigned to a group for INVESTIGATION. The group attempts to obtain further information about the case. If further information becomes available or if the authorities fail to provide adequate information to justify the prisoner's detention, the case may be changed to ADOPTION. But some cases do remain INVESTIGATION cases, even for long periods, because insufficient information is available on which to base a decision to adopt the individual as a prisoner of conscience. Even if more facts cannot be obtained, persistent inquiries on behalf of such prisoners can often help to protect them and to remind the authorities that there is international interest in their cases. It should be noted that, according to an International Council decision, AI is not bound to accept a government's opinion as to whether a prisoner has or has not used or advocated violence.

Some cases are taken up for INVESTI-GATION because the prisoners are held on politically related grounds without charge or without trial or because they have been convicted in proceedings that did not conform to internationally recognized norms. AI urges the authorities to respect the prisoners' rights to a fair trial and in the case of those detained arbitrarily to bring charges against them or release them.

Three rules safeguard AI's impartiality in its case work:

1. Groups work simultaneously for prisoners held in countries with different political and social systems.
2. Groups do not work on behalf of prisoners held by the groups' own governments. This reflects the emphasis on international responsibility for the protection of human rights.
3. Groups are not asked to work for the release of anyone whose imprisonment can be reasonably attributed to the use or advocacy of violence on his or her part or to espionage. This reinforces the distinction between prisoners of conscience (the only category of prisoner for which AI seeks unconditional release) and other prisoners (for whom AI seeks fair trials or protection against torture and execution) and ensures that AI cannot justifiably be accused of supporting "terrorism". AI applies this distinction in all cases and all countries, irrespective of political considerations. For a detailed analysis of this question, see Chapter 11, "AI and the Use of Violence".

AI has been part of the worldwide effort to get conscientious objection to military service recognized as inherent in the fundamental human right to freedom of conscience. The Statute states that "every person has the right freely to hold and to express his or her convictions and the obligation to extend a like freedom to others". This principle includes the right of a person to refuse military service on the grounds of conscience or personal conviction, without incurring any legal or physical penalty. Anyone who is imprisoned for exercising this right is considered by AI to be a prisoner of conscience. International guidelines on the

adoption of such prisoners are included in Chapter 11.

# Political trials

Political prisoners in many countries are convicted in trials that violate internationally agreed standards, or are held for years, sometimes decades, without any trial at all.

AI strives to ensure that *all* political prisoners are given a fair trial within a reasonable period of time, not just prisoners of conscience, whose release is sought regardless of criminal proceedings. While the term "prisoner of conscience" is strictly defined, the term "political prisoner" applies to anyone who is imprisoned where there is a political element in the case. When political prisoners (suspected members of opposition groups that use violence, for instance) are not necessarily prisoners of conscience, AI urges that they be given a fair trial within a reasonable period, or, if charges are not brought, released.

AI bases its work for fair trials in such cases on internationally recognized standards that require:

— the provision of defence lawyers of the prisoners' choosing;
— full prior consultation with defence counsel;
— open trial in the presence of outside observers;
— the testimony of defence witnesses and right of cross-examination;
— the repudiation of evidence extracted under duress or torture.

In situations where administrative detention is used AI goes beyond work on behalf of individuals and presses for a general amnesty for all political detainees (if prisoners of conscience would benefit), for measures to ensure detainees fair and prompt trials or for repeal of the legislation under which they are held. Situations involving mass detention without trial are often the subject of AI reports.

Where trial procedures are notoriously unjust, as in military courts that try and sentence civilians who have no right of appeal or when the defendant is denied free access to legal counsel, or when the legislation under which prisoners of conscience are detained is itself a violation of the Universal Declaration of Human Rights, AI highlights this in its reports as well as in representations to the governments concerned.

In its work for fair trials AI may send lawyers from other countries to observe and assess political trials. In some instances cases of political prisoners convicted after unfair trials are assigned to AI groups for INVESTIGATION as are cases of prisoners detained for long periods without trial.

When prisoners of conscience or individuals who are likely to become prisoners of conscience have difficulty obtaining the assistance of competent lawyers, AI looks into the possibility of providing legal aid. In countries where this is a problem on a large scale, AI may discuss the entire question of legal aid with the government and with appropriate bodies in the country, such as bar associations.

# Torture

Torture today is systematic in many parts of the world despite the international agreements that forbid it and despite the many denials from governments that use it.

Torture knows no geographical boundaries, nor can it be ascribed to any one political ideology or economic system. The list of modern torture techniques includes not only the use of archaic instruments like whips, clubs and thumbscrews but also of the contemporary technology of electricity, sophisticated methods of psychological assault and drugs that can cause dread, hallucinations, muscle spasms and paralysis.

Torture is used as a means of gaining information, of forcing confessions and of intimidating the population. Whatever its immediate purpose, torture humiliates the victim and dehumanizes the torturer. It is one of the ultimate human corruptions.

Those who justify torture argue that a lesser evil can be used to combat a greater. In the case

This secret photograph of a Latin American torture victim hanging by his wrists was sent to AI by a military officer as evidence of systematic cruelty inflicted on prisoners.

of torture, however, experience leads AI to a very different conclusion. Torture, once tolerated, becomes routine and ultimately a semi-clandestine political institution, often spreading from country to country.

To combat torture, AI has launched a worldwide Campaign for the Abolition of Torture. It has concentrated its efforts on two major fronts: (i) intervention to rescue torture victims when details are available and (ii) mobilization of international public opinion and organizations to provide long-term protection from torture. Details of the campaign are included in Chapter 4.

# The Death Penalty

AI opposes the death penalty on the grounds that it constitutes a cruel, inhuman and degrading punishment and is a violation of the right to life proclaimed in the Universal Declaration of Human Rights and other international standards. It is irrevocable; it can be inflicted on the innocent; it is brutalizing to all involved. Execution is an act of violence, and violence tends to provoke violence. The death penalty has historically claimed large numbers of victims from racial, ethnic, religious and minority groups. It has never been shown to have a special deterrent effect on violent crime.

The United Nations General Assembly has declared that it is desirable to abolish the death penalty in all cases and that the crimes to which it applies should be progressively reduced. In line with this position, widely accepted international standards state that it should be imposed only for the gravest crimes, and should not be introduced for crimes to which it does not already apply.

However, a number of United Nations member states have, on the contrary, actually increased the number of offences punishable by death. Disturbing departures from international standards have included denials of the right to appeal in death penalty cases, or to petition for clemency. Executions have frequently taken place within hours of the death sentences being passed, leaving no time for the defendants to lodge

appeals or seek clemency. This has often happened after trials in which the rights of the defence have been severely restricted.

AI keeps a log of all known death sentences and executions throughout the world. It has a network of coordinators who organize publicity and campaign for the abolition of this inhuman punishment. Whenever possible, campaigns are launched to stop threatened executions and in a number of countries AI members are urging their own government to repeal the death penalty — an issue on which AI members have the right to campaign in their own country.

# Political killings by governments

Hundreds of thousands of people during the past decade have been the victims of deliberate killings carried out on the orders of governments or with their complicity.

The killings are the work of regular military and police forces, of special units created to function without normal supervision, of "death squads" operating with government complicity and of assassins whose victims are selected targets in other countries.

A pattern of such killings — known as "extrajudicial executions" — is often accompanied by the suspension of constitutional rights, an erosion of the independence of the judiciary, intimidation of witnesses, suppression of evidence and failure to act on the results of independent investigations. Governments often deny that the killings have taken place or that their agents were involved. They may blame the deaths on opposition groups or try to pass them off as the result of armed encounters with government forces or say that the victims were killed while trying to escape from custody.

Governments are responsible, however, under national and international law for the lives and security of their citizens. They have a duty not to commit or condone political killings and to take all legislative, executive and judicial measures necessary to ensure that those responsible — directly or indirectly — are brought to justice. Their accountability is not diminished by national security considerations or by the fact that opposition groups commit similar abhorrent acts.

The term "extrajudicial executions" is used by AI for such killings in order to distinguish them from the judicial death penalty — a sentence imposed by a court after a prisoner has been convicted of a crime for which this penalty is provided by law. It also distinguishes such killings from deaths caused by the use of reasonable force in police operations, as permitted by national and international legal standards, and from killings in armed conflict.

AI has frequently campaigned to expose and halt political killings by governments in a range of countries. In 1982 an international conference was convened by the Dutch Section of AI to plan an international campaign. AI later organized a worldwide campaign to publicize killings and increase the pressure on governments to take the necessary steps to stop them.

## "Disappearances"

During recent years "disappearances" have become a cause for increasing concern. The term "disappearance" is used when people are arrested or kidnapped by government agents or by other groups directly or indirectly supported by the government and the government subsequently refuses to acknowledge that they have been seized and detained.

Victims of illegal detention often run the risk of being tortured and killed.

AI considers "disappearances" a gross violation of fundamental human rights, frequently involving not only detention without charge or trial but also torture, cruel, inhuman and degrading treatment or punishment and extrajudicial execution. It has made consistent efforts to publicize "disappearances", campaign on behalf of the victims and raise the issue at the United Nations.

"Disappearance" cases are allocated, where possible, to AI groups who then make regular inquiries of the appropriate authorities about the prisoners' whereabouts and often keep in touch with the missing people's families.

## Prison conditions

Many prisoners are kept in cramped, overcrowded and grossly inadequate conditions. In some cases this may be done deliberately to demoralize the prisoners; in others, it may constitute an additional punishment imposed by the prison authorities, such as prolonged solitary confinement.

Although AI is not a general penal reform organization, in the course of its regular case work it frequently asks for prisoners to be allowed to see a doctor or lawyer, to have visits from relatives, or to be permitted to read, study, write letters and take exercise. AI reports the conditions in which political prisoners are held in

Behind the prison walls in many countries, inmates are held in appalling conditions.

particular countries and makes representations to governments. The membership has also been involved in campaigns or long-term programs to draw public attention to conditions in particular prisons and seek improvements. AI does not, however, seek to duplicate the efforts of other bodies more specifically concerned with prison inspection, such as the International Committee of the Red Cross.

The basis for AI's work for proper prison conditions is the United Nations Standard Minimum Rules for the Treatment of Prisoners. This document, adopted by the First United Nations Congress on the Prevention of Crime and the Treatment of Offenders, lays down 95 provisions covering basic requirements for the proper treatment of prisoners. The rules cover such items as the availability of medical services, regulations for discipline and punishment, use of restraining implements and complaints procedures open to prisoners. A special section (Rules 84-93) deals with the conditions of prisoners awaiting trial.

At an international level, AI makes submissions to the five-yearly United Nations Congress on the Prevention of Crime and the Treatment of

Offenders — the body responsible for issuing and reviewing the Standard Minimum Rules.

# Refugees

The Statute of AI commits the movement to providing "financial and other relief to Prisoners of Conscience and their dependants and to persons who have lately been Prisoners of Conscience or who might reasonably be expected to be Prisoners of Conscience or to become Prisoners of Conscience if convicted or if they were to return to their own countries, and to the dependants of such persons" (Article 2).

AI opposes the sending of individuals from one country to another where they can reasonably be expected to become prisoners of conscience or to be subjected to torture, the death penalty or extrajudicial execution. In addition assistance may be given for people to emigrate, if they want to, to another country from the one where they are being held as prisoners of conscience or can reasonably be expected to become prisoners of

conscience soon or to be subjected to torture or extrajudicial execution. AI does not recognize that emigration (voluntary or involuntary) is an acceptable alternative to the release of prisoners of conscience. AI is also opposed to the release of prisoners by exchange and takes no part in arranging such trade in human beings.

AI is often asked to help refugees from one country who are detained in another. In this case, AI applies its normal investigation and adoption procedures. AI is also asked to help political refugees who face deportation back to their country of origin. In these cases, the local AI section tries to ensure that the refugee in question is guaranteed the right of appeal against deportation. An AI section, in consultation with the International Secretariat, may ask its country's government to grant asylum on humanitarian grounds. It may attest that refugees might lose their freedom if obliged to return home.

AI is a member of the Co-ordinating Committee on Assistance to Refugees of the Organization of African Unity. It also maintains contact with the United Nations High Commissioner for Refugees.

## Our freedom in defence of theirs

It is clear that the postcards, telegrams and parcels are getting through. More and more requests are received from prisoners and their families and lawyers who believe help from AI will make a difference. Letters come back, many of them smuggled out of prison or past airport censors.

The same week that a young law student was sentenced to three years' imprisonment in an Eastern European country—he had been arrested after collecting signatures calling for the release of political prisoners—his father wrote to AI:

*"I experienced the blessing of your appeal, for you have raised your voice in defence of my son. . . . Amnesty International is a light in our time, particularly for those on whose eyes darkness has fallen, when the prison doors close behind them. By your selfless work this light shines on the ever-widening circle of those who need it."*

Among the many other victims was a teacher in Latin America. While he was being tortured by the police they opened a telephone line between the torture chamber and the prisoner's home, forcing his wife to listen to her husband's screams. During that ordeal she died of a heart attack. The prisoner himself survived and was eventually allowed to go into exile with his children. He told us:

*"They killed my wife. They would have killed me too; but you intervened and saved my life."*

Some prisoners are released soon after their case is taken up; some are freed in general amnesties; others serve their entire sentences before regaining their freedom. AI, however, does not claim credit for the release of any prisoner. This is regardless of whether it has been investigating the case or campaigning for the prisoner's freedom. But once a case *is* taken up for adoption, Amnesty International never gives up its efforts.

# Chapter 4

# How Amnesty International Works

## Research

RESEARCH is central to AI's entire work. The Research Department of the International Secretariat collects and analyses information about violations of human rights around the world and keeps comprehensive records of known or possible prisoners of conscience, political prisoners, torture victims and individuals facing the death sentence.

Information comes in from many sources, public and private, and is carefully studied and cross-checked before any action is taken. Accuracy and impartiality are the twin principles that guide all AI research. Care is taken to distinguish between allegations and facts. Each new piece of information is evaluated and the reliability of the source examined. Before any information can be issued by AI it is subject to a series of checks within the International Secretariat to ensure that it conforms to the organization's policies and research standards. Similarly, care is taken to ensure impartiality. AI's purpose is not to condemn governments as such or political systems; nor does it support the views of the prisoners whose rights it seeks to protect. The research is strictly about human rights, irrespective of political considerations. To help guard against political bias, staff in the International Secretariat are not responsible for work on their own countries.

As a result of years of painstaking, thorough research since 1961 AI is now widely used as an international resource centre by scholars, journalists, governments and organizations seeking information on political imprisonment and related violations of human rights.

Research is only the first stage in AI's work. The information becomes the basis of action on behalf of individual prisoners of conscience and other victims. Suggestions for action are sent out by the International Secretariat to AI's worldwide network of members, groups and supporters.

## Case work

AI's global impartiality is translated into a system of group work. Each group is assigned the cases of at least two prisoners from contrasting political and geographical backgrounds and assumes responsibility for working on their behalf. If the group has received an investigation case, it must begin making inquiries about the prisoner. This usually involves writing to various government ministries. A constant stream of letters may be needed and often the group must be prepared to work for months or even years. If the group is allocated cases of prisoners of conscience, the members must begin campaigning for their release. This will involve sending appeals to the government, writing letters to the prison authorities, visiting embassies (coordinated through the section), organizing petitions and public activities. The group may also be put in touch with the prisoners' families and may try to raise money to help them with legal fees or medical costs.

According to the nature of the case, the group may have to take up a number of issues. It may try to protect the prisoner from torture in detention.

It may have to press for the prisoner's rights to legal advice and family visits, to a fair trial (including a defence counsel of the prisoner's choosing) and to appeal. If the prisoner is sentenced to death, the group campaigns to prevent his or her execution. It may also be concerned about the victim's prison conditions and may need to urge the authorities to allow the prisoner medical care and visits and permission to write letters and take exercise.

In many countries where arbitrary detention of political suspects has taken place on a massive scale, AI's case work can affect only a small proportion of the prison population — although it does help to highlight the plight of the many hundreds whose names may never be known. More wide-ranging techniques have been developed to bring pressure on governments responsible for systematic and widespread human rights abuses. These techniques supplement the work for individual prisoners and the two approaches are combined where this is thought to best serve the prisoners' interests.

A detailed account of AI's case work is given in Chapter 9.

## Campaigns

AI's campaigns help to focus public attention on various aspects of political imprisonment. The campaigning is wide-ranging and varied: some campaigns — such as those for the abolition of torture and the death penalty — keep up the pressure on issues of long-term concern; other, shorter campaigns concentrate on human rights abuses in certain countries or on groups of political prisoners.

Other campaigns may be organized by AI sections on particular issues in their own countries. Although members may not take up individual cases in their own countries, they may become involved in campaigns to repeal death penalty legislation or to urge their own government to ratify the international human rights covenants.

## Campaign for the Abolition of Torture

The abolition of torture has always been one of AI's goals. By the early 1970s AI had amassed overwhelming evidence that torture was being inflicted by many governments on political op-

> ## OUR MANDATE
> - Secure the immediate and unconditional release of all prisoners of conscience.
> - Ensure fair and prompt trials for all political prisoners.
> - Abolish torture and executions.
>
> ## OUR CAMPAIGN
> - Human rights are a human responsibility. Whenever they are violated, people are the victims. They and their families need practical help.
> - Through its network of members and supporters, Amnesty International takes up individual cases, mobilizes public opinion and seeks improved international standards for the treatment of prisoners.
> - You can find out more about Amnesty International, including the addresses of our local groups and sections, by writing to:
>
> **AMNESTY INTERNATIONAL
> INTERNATIONAL SECRETARIAT
> LONDON, UNITED KINGDOM**

ponents and that this practice was increasing to the extent that it could be termed an "epidemic".

Accordingly, in 1972 AI's International Council launched a Campaign for the Abolition of Torture intended to rouse public opinion and mobilize people internationally against torture. The campaign's first year culminated in the December 1973 Conference for the Abolition of Torture and the presentation to the President of the United Nations General Assembly of an appeal to outlaw torture signed by more than one million people from 90 countries. The evidence from AI's research files provided ample material for a 1973 AI *Report on Torture*, revised in 1975, which presented the evidence of torture over the previous decade.

Opposing torture is part of the regular program of the International Secretariat, which monitors allegations of torture and initiates actions to stop the practice. These efforts have been aided by special studies ranging from long-term medical research into the effects of electric torture, papers on the legal implications of behaviour modification techniques and investigations of torture in various countries.

The campaign aims primarily to stimulate international action to halt torture and rescue victims. Since the Conference for the Abolition of Torture, AI has worked with sympathetic governments, intergovernmental and non-governmental organizations on an international strategy to outlaw and prevent torture. The first major success was achieved on 9 December 1975 when the United Nations General Assembly adopted by acclamation Resolution 3452 (XXX) which brought into international law a historic Declaration on the Protection of All Persons from Torture or Other Cruel, Inhuman or Degrading Treatment or Punishment. The 12-article declaration defines torture and gives guidelines for all states, including the stipulation that they must ensure that torture is a criminal offence and that any statement obtained through torture or similar ill-treatment "may not be invoked as evidence against the person concerned or against any other person in any proceedings".

AI is now seeking the adoption by the United Nations of an effective international convention against torture. Unlike the declaration against torture, the convention would be legally binding on states.

AI realizes, however, that action merely on this level cannot achieve the eradication of torture. The movement's activities include:

— urgent worldwide appeals on behalf of victims of torture;
— support for the rehabilitation of torture victims;
— publicity about torture through reports, statements to the international news media and international campaigns about torture in particular countries;
— mobilization of professional, religious, medical, trade union and other national, regional and international bodies in the struggle against torture.

AI members receive regular appeals in the monthly *Amnesty International Newsletter* on behalf of torture victims. They are asked to send letters to the appropriate government officials urging humane treatment for prisoners in their custody. They can also participate in the worldwide Urgent Action network that tries to prevent the torture of people who have been taken into custody.

The campaign has been helped by the development of AI medical groups. Assisted by a Medical Advisory Board, established in 1977, medical groups in some 30 countries have participated in work on behalf of torture victims (including the examination of such people from many countries) and published reports on their findings.

As part of its long-term campaign strategy, AI is also trying to get codes of ethics established for jurists, medical practitioners, police, military personnel and others who may become involved in torture. A number of such codes have been either drafted or adopted by professional bodies. A collection of these, *Codes of Professional Ethics*, has been published by AI.

"**Damn these Amnesty letters—the international market for thumbscrews has collapsed . . .**"

# Program for the Abolition of the Death Penalty

The fact that people were being executed because their religion or opinions were unacceptable to their government was highlighted in the appeal that first launched the AI movement. Concern about the death penalty has frequently featured in AI's work over the years. As the movement has developed so has its mandate, particularly in response to evidence of the cruel, inhuman and degrading treatment of prisoners. In a series of decisions in the early 1970s the International Council resolved to oppose torture and the death penalty in all cases. It decided in 1974 to intensify its efforts for the total abolition of the death penalty — a decision reaffirmed in more recent council decisions.

On Human Rights Day 1977 AI held an international Conference on the Death Penalty in Stockholm. The participants included lawyers, judges, politicians, psychologists, police officials, penologists, theologians and journalists from more than 50 countries. The conference adopted the Declaration of Stockholm (see Chapter 11). It declared its total and unconditional opposition to the death penalty. It condemned executions, in whatever form, committed or condoned by governments. It affirmed that executions as a means of political coercion, whether by government agencies or others, are equally unacceptable. The Stockholm Declaration was adopted by AI in March 1978 as a statement of principle on the abolition of the death penalty.

In September 1979 a major AI report, *The Death Penalty*, was published giving details about death penalty legislation and practice in 134 countries, as well as arguments in favour of abolition.

In addition to these general initiatives, AI has developed a regular worldwide program for the eradication of the death penalty, regardless of the crimes for which it is imposed. The program includes:

— urgent action or other appeals to the head of state when a death sentence is about to be carried out;
— public AI statements deploring the use of the death penalty and urging clemency;
— long-term work by AI groups on countries where the death penalty is in force;
— short-term actions on specific countries focusing on the death penalty and urging changes in legislation;
— publicity and lobbying by sections within their own countries to change legislation or to prevent reintroduction of the death penalty.

AI has persistently urged United Nations member states to support moves to abolish the death penalty. In August 1980 AI backed a resolution submitted by 42 non-governmental organizations to the Sixth United Nations Congress on the Prevention of Crime and the Treatment of Offenders. The resolution called on governments to stop using the death penalty and urged the United Nations General Assembly to promulgate a declaration that would urge its worldwide abolition. In October 1980 AI presented to the Secretary-General of the United Nations and the President of the General Assembly an appeal calling on the United Nations and its member states to take all necessary steps for the immediate and total abolition of the death penalty throughout the world. The appeal was signed by people in more than 100 countries including internationally prominent politicians, government ministers, religious and labour leaders, police and prison officers, scientists, doctors, artists and writers.

# Urgent Actions

AI has to be able to act quickly to stop torture and save lives. To do this it has developed a network of volunteers throughout the world who are ready to send immediate appeals in emergency cases. This Urgent Action technique was first developed to help people threatened with torture. It has since been extended to other cases which demand immediate worldwide action.

Since the middle of 1976 Urgent Action appeals have been issued on behalf of victims and potential victims of torture, in cases of "disappearance", on behalf of individuals under sentence of death, of prisoners needing medical treatment, of prisoners on hunger-strike (when their demands fall within AI's mandate) and at critical stages in trials.

Urgent Action appeals are telexed and mailed from the International Secretariat to Urgent Action coordinators in different countries who then send the appeal to groups or individuals. Urgent Action participants are asked to send telegrams or letters to the authorities in the country concerned. When appropriate, appeals by specialist groups, such as health workers, lawyers or trade unionists, are requested.

Further information on Urgent Action appeals is given regularly to Urgent Action coordinators who in turn pass it on to those who participated in the original Urgent Action. If the situation remains unchanged or has deteriorated, or if no new information has been received, further appeals are requested. However, in nearly half the cases some change is reported: acknowledgement of detention, release, transfer to hospital or commutation of a death sentence.

## Campaign for Prisoners of the Month

Every month the International Secretariat chooses three cases of prisoners of conscience — each of them already adopted by one or more groups — for this special campaign. The prisoners may be extremely ill or may have been detained in severe conditions for a very long time; they may be representative of a group of prisoners needing extra efforts on their behalf. The details of these cases are included in the *Amnesty International Newsletter* and sent to AI members and sub-scribers for immediate action. The three cases are carefully selected so as to reflect the political balance of AI's work.

Details of the three cases include addresses for letters on the prisoners' behalf. Members may prefer to send their appeals to the relevant embassies in their own country, these letters usually then being forwarded by the embassy to the authorities in the prisoners' country.

Among the actions which you can take on behalf of the prisoners are:

**1. Writing individual letters** — you can send brief letters to the appropriate government authorities appealing for the prisoners' release. You should do this as soon as you receive the *Newsletter* and avoid expressing yourself in a way that might be construed as aggressive or prejudiced.

**2. Organizing petitions** — you can prepare petitions on behalf of each of the prisoners and circulate them for signature among friends, professional colleagues and other people interested in human rights.

**3. Arranging mass letter writing** —where possible, you can send details about the cases to other organizations or circulate them among the general public with a request for letters to be sent on behalf of the prisoners.

"This new policy of liberalization has sabotaged my stamp collection. In the old days when we had prisoners we used to get letters from all over the world".

You can seek the support of prominent citizens in your community and ask them to participate regularly in the campaign.

**4. Creating publicity** — your local AI group can encourage the local press to publish details of the cases each month so that a wider protest can be generated. The group can also ask sympathetic institutions to publish the facts about the cases in their monthly bulletins or newsletters so that their members can add their voices to the protest.

**5. Holding public meetings** — your local AI group can hold a public meeting once a month to publicize the critical cases and to focus attention on the work of the AI movement. A formal resolution can be sent by the meeting to the appropriate authorities on behalf of each of the three prisoners, or everyone can be asked to write an individual letter on behalf of the prisoners.

**6. Increasing awareness about human rights** — the monthly campaign is an excellent way to raise basic human rights issues in any community and has been used effectively in various countries by teachers, social workers and editors to increase public awareness about human rights.

# Prisoners of Conscience Week

No case of political imprisonment is typical. Each is an instance of acute personal suffering—of a human being detained unjustly, removed from normal life by the failure of governments to respect universal human rights standards.

Every year the International Secretariat selects prisoner cases for special action during Prisoners of Conscience Week in October. The International Council may decide on a particular human rights theme to be illustrated by the cases.

During Prisoners of Conscience Week AI members conduct special programs on behalf of such prisoners. Feature articles on them are written for the local press and other publications. Special events are organized by groups and sections: concerts, plays about freedom or political imprisonment, public meetings, poster displays — to attract people to the living work of AI and to raise funds and recruit new members.

# Country campaigns and special actions

Political imprisonment, detention without trial, torture and executions cannot be confronted solely by highlighting individual prisoner cases. Much of AI's work, both national and international, draws attention to patterns of human rights violations and puts pressure on governments to stop these abuses.

Campaigns on these issues include organizing petitions, generating publicity, holding public meetings and lobbying professional associations and elected representatives. All these activities aim to get the government authorities to respect international human rights standards. The campaigns are coordinated by the International Secretariat working with a network of campaign coordinators in the sections. Hundreds of local groups participate in each international campaign — there are normally two or three each year.

As well as these large campaigns, AI often organizes "special actions" on matters such as repressive laws and the treatment of prisoners in particular countries. The number of groups taking part in these more limited actions varies, although, like major campaigns, they too are coordinated by the International Secretariat and section coordinators.

# Regional Action Networks

Groups may also participate in regional action networks. These involve AI action on a particular region or group of countries where there is a pattern of human rights violations of AI concern which cannot be dealt with only by long-term case work for individual prisoners or the urgent action scheme. The networks are designed to make it possible for AI members to act quickly on cases of short-term detention, "disappearances", executions and other abuses of human rights. In some regions, there is also a need for action on general concerns such as prison conditions or legislation. Groups in a network may also be asked to assist the IS in seeking information about specific cases that are not yet taken up for adoption or investigation.

The networks are made up of groups in different sections. The background information and requests for action are prepared by the International Secretariat and distributed to groups via the appointed coordinator at national level. Participation in a regional action network is one of the additional long-term activities that groups can enlist in — to complement their work on individual cases from other regions.

# Missions

AI frequently sends experienced lawyers, other experts in the field of human rights and its own officials on missions to various countries and conferences to represent the organization, or to collect on-the-spot information about prisoners of conscience, legal procedures and other matters with which it is concerned. AI missions are also sent to observe important or political trials.

All missions must be authorized by the International Executive Committee, and the authorities concerned are notified. A report of each mission is subsequently made to the International Executive Committee. The report is normally submitted to the government for comment before publication.

Missions on behalf of individual prisoners of conscience and visits to prisoners adopted by AI are discussed in Chapter 9.

## Relief

Prisoners are not the only ones to suffer the effects of imprisonment. A family whose breadwinner has been imprisoned, perhaps detained for a number of years without trial, faces many hardships. Paying for food, school fees, rent and travel may become an insuperable problem. Help, either from an AI group or from general funds held at the International Secretariat, can make a great difference.

In one country, the money may cover the fare for a wife to visit her imprisoned husband. In another, it may help meet the family's living costs. Relief funds may help the prisoner directly, enabling him or her in some instances to buy the few small luxuries prisoners are allowed, or basic necessities such as blankets and winter clothes in cold climates. Relief is not intended, however, to compensate the prisoners or their families for total loss of income during the period of detention.

Relief funds can also help the rehabilitation of former prisoners. In certain cases it may be used for medical care after torture.

In carrying out this humanitarian work, which is governed by the same principles of impartiality and political balance that guide the overall work of AI, the organization relies heavily on the generosity of its members and on individual donors. The many letters sent to AI by prisoners and their families attest to the importance of AI's relief program.

The way relief is sent to prisoners and their families varies from country to country. In some instances centralized relief programs are organized by the International Secretariat; in others, groups send gifts or money direct.

Relief procedures are described in detail in Chapter 9.

## Publicity and Publications

Publicity is one of AI's most powerful tools. Sometimes a vigorous local publicity campaign by an AI group has turned into a national protest and made a distinct impact on a government. The pressure of public indignation *can* make officials reassess their policies. In many countries publicity abroad has helped lead to the granting of amnesties, improved prison conditions, open trials and the commutation of death sentences.

Worldwide publicity is generated by news releases and the publication of reports. The International Secretariat is responsible for their preparation and production. The major publication is the annual report which gives a country-by-country summary of the previous year's work. It also describes AI's initiatives in the field of international organizations and its programs for the abolition of torture and the death penalty.

Other publications include mission reports, studies of individual countries and of broader issues such as torture, the death penalty and political killings by governments. The International Secretariat also provides a monthly *Amnesty International Newsletter*. This is a bulletin which contains news of AI concerns in individual countries, special feature articles and the Campaign for Prisoners of the Month.

AI sections also publish reports and newsletters, many of which are translations of documents issued by the International Secretariat. Guidelines on publicity and publications for sections and groups are outlined in Chapter 7.

## Representations to National Governments

AI sections have become increasingly conscious of the need to make representations to their own governments about AI concerns: guarantees of asylum for political refugees, diplomatic intervention on behalf of political prisoners in other countries, support for initiatives in international human rights law in bodies like the United Nations, human rights issues as they affect trade and cultural relations, human rights education in police, military and medical training programs, changes in laws on the death penalty and refugees.

AI sections and groups are not authorized, however, to make representations to their own governments about violations of human rights in their own countries, except in the case of laws that provide for the death penalty. The rules on sections' work on their own countries are reproduced in Chapter 11.

# The United Nations and International Organizations

AI's work is based on the belief that the protection of human rights is an international responsibility. It seeks the universal application of internationally agreed human rights standards. Work at the United Nations and with other intergovernmental and non-governmental organizations is therefore an important aspect of the movement's efforts to develop international standards and to strengthen the machinery for ensuring that they are respected by governments.

AI is represented at the United Nations by officers in New York, Geneva and Vienna. It is represented also at UNESCO in Paris. It has consultative status with the United Nations Economic and Social Council (ECOSOC) and may therefore make representations in certain ECOSOC committees. It contributes to the work of the United Nations Commission on Human Rights and AI representatives attend most of its sessions in Geneva. On 10 December 1978 AI received the United Nations Human Rights Prize for "outstanding contributions in the field of human rights".

AI has representatives also in Strasbourg (for the Council of Europe), Brussels (for the European Communities), and New York (for the Organization of American States).

AI sections are often asked by the International Secretariat to make AI's concerns known to their countries' representatives to the United Nations and other international bodies. Details on international human rights standards and AI's work with international organizations are given in Chapter 12.

# Target Sector Work

The professions, trade unions and other groups in the community with special interests, skills or influence are frequently approached by AI for support. This is called "target sector work".

Trade unionists, journalists, academics, members of the medical professions, religious bodies, women's groups, youth organizations, teachers and many others contribute to AI's work either as individuals or through their organizations. They are often asked by AI members to join in letter writing campaigns on behalf of particular individuals — for example, members of their profession or social group — who are the victims of political imprisonment, torture or other violations of human rights. Some organizations join AI's country campaigns and special actions or participate in the programs against torture, "disappearances", the death penalty and political killings by governments.

Many sections have appointed coordinators to organize relations with target sectors, in particular trade unions, religious groups, educational institutions and others involved in commercial, financial, cultural, military or security relations with other countries.

In some sections professional people have joined AI and formed "professional groups". There are extensive networks of AI medical and lawyers groups, and a growing number of teachers groups, journalists groups, and all-party parliamentary groups. They join in the work on behalf of individual prisoners and in general campaigns, and help strengthen links between AI and their professional associations.

AI medical groups help their sections to organize campaigns on behalf of prisoners in poor health and examine and treat victims of torture and ex-prisoners in need of medical care. They approach medical organizations in their own country, raise AI concerns at medical congresses and work for the adoption and implementation of codes of ethics for medical personnel who may be involved in torture.

Lawyers groups participate in appeals for individual prisoners and general campaigns where their legal expertise can be especially useful. Their contribution can make a particular impact when AI takes up judicial and legislative issues with governments, in cases of political prisoners who have been denied a fair trial or been subjected to torture. Lawyers groups also advise AI sections about a variety of legal matters and help draw the attention of the legal profession in their countries to human rights abuses in countries around the world.

AI needs the support of organized labour: the movement has established relations with trade unions and involved trade unionists individually and collectively in campaigns and case work.

Numerous religious bodies — representing a wide range of creeds and denominations — support AI. Many sections and local groups have established good working relations with representatives of various religious communities in their countries or localities.

Commercial relations are a particular aspect of target sector work. Approaching companies and other bodies and individuals influential in the commercial world is more complex than working with many other target sectors. AI regularly gives information to companies and governments about human rights violations in countries with which they have commercial relations. However, it does not address itself to the general economic system in those countries, does not draw political conclusions from its work for human rights and refrains from calling for sanctions, such as boycotts, against governments abusing human rights. Furthermore, AI takes no stand on the legitimacy of the commercial relations themselves or on the responsibility for such abuses by companies or others on the basis simply of their having commercial relations with the countries concerned.

Similar principles apply when approaching institutions and governments operating in military, security and police spheres. In certain cases, action can be taken by AI on military, security and police transfers to governments. Such action, including calling for a cessation of the transfer, can be taken when these transfers are known to facilitate violations of the human rights with which AI is concerned. Specific authorization by the International Executive Committee is necessary in such cases.

# Human Rights Education

AI wants to increase public awareness of human rights and the involvement of AI members in educational programs has become increasingly important.

Many sections are helping to introduce courses on human rights in schools, colleges and adult evening classes. Teaching kits on AI and other educational materials include general literature and articles about human rights issues to stimulate discussion (such as a course on "Prison Literature") and facts about human rights violations. In some programs school children are asked to write letters on behalf of individual prisoners of conscience. In this way they can come to understand the problems AI deals with and how AI works.

In many sections teachers groups have been established to explore the possibilities of introducing courses on human rights into school curricula, cooperating with national educational institutions, teachers trade unions and educational associations.

# Chapter 5

# Amnesty International throughout the world

AI is a movement of active volunteer members throughout the world. They may belong to formal AI bodies, such as sections and groups, or they may support AI activities as individual members or subscribers.

## Members and subscribers

AI has more than 350,000 members, subscribers and supporters in over 150 countries and territories (1982 statistics). They come from all walks of life and include social workers, lawyers, teachers, trade unionists, homemakers, students, journalists, doctors, nurses, retired people, artists, clergy, veterans, labourers, politicians, farmers, and so forth. The movement is open to anyone who supports its goals.

Most AI activists belong to local groups but in some sections there are many who are not necessarily involved in group activities. These individuals participate in the Campaign for Prisoners of the Month by sending letters on behalf of prisoners of conscience whose cases feature in the monthly *Amnesty International Newsletter*. They may also take part in Urgent Action appeals — sending letters and telegrams in an effort to stop torture and executions. Members and subscribers may also contribute to fundraising and publicity drives, selling and distributing AI publications, helping to recruit new members and carrying the AI message to professional groups that may be willing to take action on behalf of imprisoned colleagues.

Individual members and subscribers in countries where there is an AI section have little direct

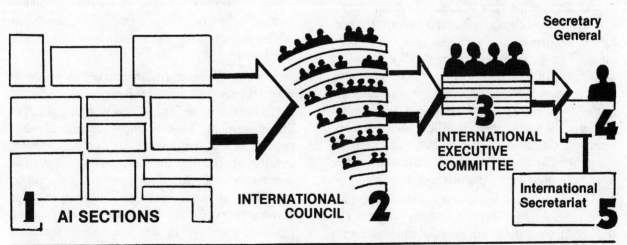

**1.** In more than 40 countries AI's membership is organized into sections with locally elected governing bodies.

**2.** Voting delegates from the sections meet at the International Council to decide the movement's policy and budget.

**3.** The International Executive Committee is elected by the Council. It governs the movement between Council meetings.

**4.** The Secretary General is appointed by the International Executive Committee to run the day-to-day affairs of AI and head the International Secretariat.

**5.** The International Secretariat collects information about prisoners, coordinates worldwide publicity and campaigns and advises the groups and members in their work.

contact with the International Secretariat.

In countries where there is no AI section, people can become individual subscribers by registering with the International Secretariat. They receive the *Amnesty International Newsletter* and are invited to participate in the Campaign for Prisoners of the Month and to support appeals in the newsletter on behalf of torture victims and prisoners facing the death penalty. Subscribers pay an annual fee determined by the International Executive Committee.

# Local AI Groups

Most of AI's active members work together in groups. From the beginning these local groups have been the basic unit of AI's structure and work. Over the years, the scope of their activities has been expanded and developed.

There are over 2,600 Amnesty International groups in more than 40 countries registered with the International Secretariat. The number of groups is steadily growing, particularly in countries outside Western Europe and North America.

These groups normally consist of between 10 and 15 active members (although many have more). One of their main tasks is to work on behalf of at least two individual prisoners. Depending on the type of case, the group seeks the prisoner's release, a fair and prompt trial or further information about the prisoner's situation. The group sends appeals direct to the authorities of the country concerned, and where appropriate generates local publicity and interest in the case. Group members may send relief to the prisoners and their families where this is required. Groups also participate in any general campaigns and special actions on human rights in the country where the prisoner is held.

Groups are expected to support the Campaign for the Abolition of Torture and the program for the abolition of the death penalty, through participation in the Urgent Action scheme or special appeals and campaigns.

Local groups represent AI in the community and seek publicity for the movement's work. They contribute to the financing of the organization by conducting fund-raising activities. The funds they raise must cover their own operating costs, provide relief for prisoners and

support the AI section in their country.

The initiative for forming a local group usually comes from a number of individuals. Each may have heard about AI from a friend or through a newspaper or public meeting. After contacting the AI office in their country or the International Secretariat they receive further information about the movement and, on request, the names of other people in their locality known to be interested in AI. After they have met and decided to apply for recognition as a group, the application is dealt with by the section office or by the International Secretariat in countries without a local section.

The section is responsible for training new groups—sometimes by sending experienced AI members to visit them or by organizing training seminars. Such groups often start work on the Campaign for Prisoners of the Month and receive Urgent Action appeals. When the section is assured that a group is able to carry the responsibility of long-term work on a prisoner dossier, the section approves the group and registers it with the International Secretariat.

All new groups should receive a copy of the *Amnesty International Handbook*, the Statute and other basic documents. Usually prisoner cases and action materials are sent to groups by the International Secretariat via their section office. (In some instances, where the section has not yet taken on this responsibility, the International Secretariat sends the material direct to the groups.)

A group is free to organize itself in whatever way it thinks most effective for its work, provided that it observes the Statute and Working Rules of the movement. Most groups appoint a chairperson, treasurer and secretary and may appoint members to handle other responsibilities such as press relations. Some groups find it useful to have one or more members taking particular responsibility for the work on behalf of each prisoner case — in order to have someone always available to deal with urgent correspondence between group meetings.

Continuity in the work of the group is essential. Provision must be made for the training of new members, proper handling of documents and correspondence and the transfer of tasks and responsibilities if group members are on holiday or have to leave the group.

Guidelines for the work of local groups are given in detail in Chapter 11.

# Sections

There are now some 40 countries where AI members are organized into formal bodies, known as sections. These are of key importance in providing networks for campaigns and case work, fund-raising and publicity. They vary considerably in size and structure: in some countries there may be a central headquarters with permanent staff, regional offices around the country, several hundred groups, and several thousand members. In others the section may consist of very few members and have limited resources.

An AI section is recognized by the International Executive Committee and is responsible for contributing to and carrying out the movement's international policy. The responsibilities include organizing the membership and fund-raising; supervising and improving group work; planning campaigns; developing contacts with the news media, professional associations, trade unions and other bodies.

All sections have an executive committee or national board elected by the members. It is responsible, either directly or through a permanent office, for coordinating and administering the activities of the AI members and groups in that country or territory.

All sections receive weekly mailings from the International Secretariat that include campaign material, requests for action, country reports and general information. They also get copies of all letters sent by the International Secretariat to any AI group in their country. Several sections are sent prisoner dossiers from the International Secretariat which they then allocate to individual groups.

The sections often produce their own newsletters for their members, incorporating articles in them from the *Amnesty International Newsletter* as well as news about their own activities. In most cases, the sections are responsible for translating AI information into their own local and national languages.

The sections may establish different kinds of groups or structures in their own countries or territories.

The extent and nature of regional structures varies from section to section. In a large country or where there is a large membership, regional structures may be based on existing regional divisions. The regional structure may be the focus for local groups and members in the area and may coordinate campaigns, training and other activities. It may also serve an administrative function as a link between the section and the local membership.

*Country Coordinators and Coordination Groups.* As sections become more experienced, they often appoint an individual or group of individuals to act as a coordinator or coordination group for work on a particular country or part of the world.

Country coordinators or coordination groups are a link between the Research Department of the International Secretariat and the local groups. They are responsible for advising the section on questions about human rights in the country or particular region and planning the work of the section's groups and members accordingly.

The appointment and establishment of country coordinators or coordination groups is the section's responsibility, in consultation with the International Secretariat. The International Council has adopted criteria for coordinators and coordination groups and spelled out the minimum tasks of such officers or groups. Any individual or group interested in country coordination work should consult their section.

*Professional Groups.* To get members of particular professions to work on behalf of prisoners of conscience and against torture and the death penalty, groups may be set up by a section to coordinate approaches to professional associations. These groups usually consist of members of the same profession, such as doctors, lawyers and teachers, who seek to involve their colleagues in AI's work. Such professional groups can assist local AI groups in their work on behalf of individual cases. For example, they can organize appeals by the relevant profession to government authorities and professional colleagues in the target country.

Some of the professional groups, in particular the medical, legal and trade union groups, are sent special material from the International Secretariat and participate in appeals and country campaigns.

# The International Council

The International Council is the supreme governing body of AI. It consists of representatives of all sections who attend both as delegates and as observers. It has the sole authority to amend the movement's Statute.

The International Council determines AI's mandate and policy. It reviews the activities of the International Executive Committee and the International Secretariat, and endorses a plan for the coming years. The Council elects eight of the nine members of the International Executive Committee, including a Treasurer (the staff of the International Secretariat elects one member from among themselves). It receives the accounts, approves the overall budget (in relation to the plan) and agrees on the annual financial contributions to be made by all sections, in accordance with their size and funding capacity.

The International Council usually lasts four and a half days and is a meeting of about 300 people. It has met every year since 1968 — each year in a different city on the invitation of one of the movement's sections. From 1983 onwards it will meet every two years.

Working parties are arranged to discuss resolutions put to the International Council by the sections and International Executive Committee. The recommendations of the working parties are then discussed and approved by the plenary session. All decisions are recorded in a report issued after the Council meeting.

# International Executive Committee

The International Council elects members to an International Executive Committee to carry out its policies. The International Executive Committee consists of nine members — seven, each from a different AI section or country, plus the Treasurer, as well as the International Secretariat staff representative. With the exception of the staff representative who serves for one year all members serve a term of two years (renewable) and can be re-elected for a maximum of three consecutive terms. The committee members themselves elect a chairperson to hold office for one year (renewable). The committee may also co-opt up to two additional non-voting members to serve until the next International Council meets.

The International Executive Committee normally meets four times a year. Each member has specific responsibilities; however, they share collective responsibility for all decisions. Subcommittees are sometimes set up to discuss particular questions and make proposals to the full committee. The committee supervises the implementation of International Council decisions and the plan adopted by the Council. It discusses and approves priorities in AI's country work, missions and approaches to governments. It approves initiatives at the United Nations and relations with other international organizations, large campaigns and budget proposals and takes major administrative decisions.

The agenda and reports of the meetings are circulated to all sections. The committee also monitors the activities of the membership, receives annual reports from sections and directs the development of the movement in new areas.

# International Committees

International committees are established by the International Council or by the International Executive Committee to advise them about particular aspects of AI's work. Members of most committees are appointed by the International Executive Committee, in consultation with sections. One member of the International Executive Committee is responsible for liaison with each of these permanent committees.

There are now five permanent international committees:

1. The *Financial Control Committee* was set up by the International Council meeting in Vienna in September 1973. It consists of three AI members and an alternate member elected by the International Council for two-year terms. It reviews the financial administration of the International Secretariat and monitors adherence to all financial procedures. It submits reports to the International Executive Committee and International Council.

2. The *Borderline Committee* comprises three people appointed by the International Executive Committee from three different sections or countries, and an alternate member from another country to act in cases concerning one of the regular members' own countries. It considers cases referred to it by the International Executive Committee for advice on whether they fulfil the statutory requirements for adoption or investigation as prisoners of conscience. All communications to the Borderline Committee are channelled through the Legal Office of the International Secretariat.

3. The *Medical Advisory Board* was established in 1977 by the International Executive Committee. It consists of four members from different sections. It advises the Committee on medical matters and, in consultation with the International Secretariat and sections, helps coordinate the development of AI medical work throughout the world.

4. An *Advisory Group on Information Handling and Technology* (InfoTech) was set up by the International Executive Committee in March 1981. It consists of four members and is responsible for advising the Committee and the International Secretariat on all aspects of information handling, including computerization.

5. The *Committee for Systematic Evaluation of Techniques* (SYSTEC) was established by the International Council in 1981 to evaluate AI's working methods. It advises the International Executive Committee and sections on techniques and studies their effectiveness as requested by the International Executive Committee and International Council.

In addition to these permanent committees other international committees may be established from time to time by the International Council or by the International Executive Committee. For example a Mandate Committee was set up by the International Council in 1978. It clarified AI's position on standards for fair trials, the definition of "prisoner of conscience", and policy on conscientious objection, sexual orientation and political killings. The committee's report was discussed, amended and adopted by the International Council in 1979.

Other special committees have examined the possibility of decentralizing AI's work and reviewed the movement's structure and its international decision-making process.

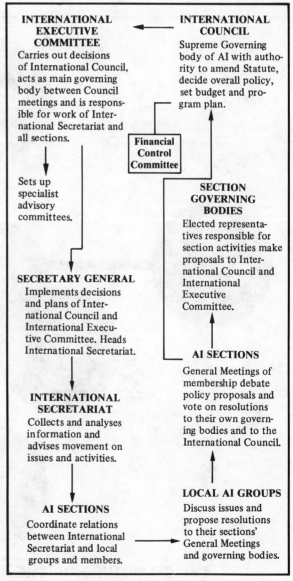

**INTERNATIONAL EXECUTIVE COMMITTEE**
Carries out decisions of International Council, acts as main governing body between Council meetings and is responsible for work of International Secretariat and all sections.

Sets up specialist advisory committees.

**SECRETARY GENERAL**
Implements decisions and plans of International Council and International Executive Committee. Heads International Secretariat.

**INTERNATIONAL SECRETARIAT**
Collects and analyses information and advises movement on issues and activities.

**AI SECTIONS**
Coordinate relations between International Secretariat and local groups and members.

**INTERNATIONAL COUNCIL**
Supreme Governing body of AI with authority to amend Statute, decide overall policy, set budget and program plan.

**Financial Control Committee**

**SECTION GOVERNING BODIES**
Elected representatives responsible for section activities make proposals to International Council and International Executive Committee.

**AI SECTIONS**
General Meetings of membership debate policy proposals and vote on resolutions to their own governing bodies and to the International Council.

**LOCAL AI GROUPS**
Discuss issues and propose resolutions to their sections' General Meetings and governing bodies.

**DECISION MAKING IN AI**

# International Secretariat

The first AI headquarters was in a lawyer's chambers in London, staffed by local volunteers. Out of this evolved the International Secretariat which now has a paid staff of some 150 people, comprising at least 20 nationalities, as well as a number of regular volunteers. The International Council has periodically questioned whether the secretariat should remain in London. After looking at a range of possibilities it has decided that it should stay there and continue to benefit from being in a city which is a convenient centre for gathering information, press contacts and diplomatic activity. There are secretariat staff also working in Colombo, New York, Paris and San José.

The secretariat is divided into five main departments which work closely together:

***Secretary General's Office.*** The Secretary General's Office (SGO) is the central point of the secretariat. The Secretary General and the Deputy Secretary General are responsible to the International Executive Committee for the organization's day-to-day work. They authorize all AI's public statements and publications and are involved in decisions about all major policy questions, diplomatic initiatives and missions.

The SGO coordinates the work of the entire International Secretariat. It organizes regular planning and administration meetings. It is responsible for servicing the International Executive Committee and all international meetings, including the International Council.

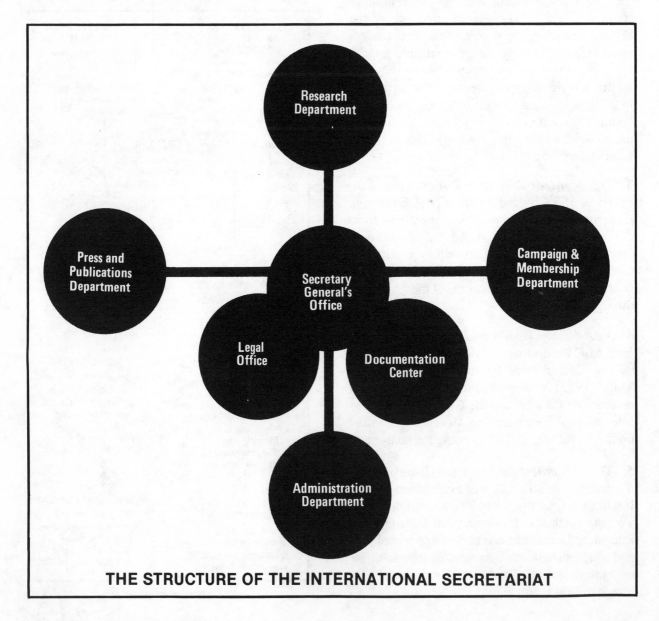

**THE STRUCTURE OF THE INTERNATIONAL SECRETARIAT**

Attached to the SGO are two specialized units, the Legal Office and the Documentation Centre.

The *Legal Office* advises the secretariat and the movement on international human rights standards and legal questions. It is responsible for relations with all international organizations and works closely with the permanent AI representatives in New York, Paris, Geneva, Strasbourg, Vienna and Brussels. It also coordinates representations made by AI sections to member states of international organizations. The Legal Office handles questions related to the interpretation of the AI Statute, reviews section statutes and coordinates submissions to the Borderline Committee.

The *Documentation Centre* is the central point for storage and retrieval of AI information; it keeps all material produced by the secretariat as well as public material from all sections. It also supplies the International Secretariat with public information related to AI objectives including press material and documentation from other organizations. It maintains AI's archives, a reference library and an audio-visual library. The centre gives advice on information systems and technology and has overall responsibility for the development of computerized programs.

*Research Department.* Nearly half the International Secretariat staff work in the Research Department. It plays the key role in collecting, verifying and analysing information on political imprisonment, torture and the death penalty throughout the world. The department has five divisions for work on Africa, the Americas, Asia, Europe and the Middle East. The Head and Deputy Head of Research are responsible for planning and quality control.

Researchers prepare the background information, strategy and briefing papers on which AI's policy, action, publicity work and diplomatic initiatives are based. The department maintains a wide network of contacts, prepares and participates in AI missions, and monitors news reports on each region.

With the help of executive assistants, researchers advise AI members on case work and campaigns. The Research Department also makes proposals for the distribution of relief to prisoners and their families.

*Campaign and Membership Department.* This part of the secretariat is responsible for liaison with AI's members throughout the world and the overall coordination of campaigns and special action networks. It is in regular contact with AI sections and with members and groups in countries where no section has yet been established. It is responsible for AI's development program in those parts of Africa, Asia, Latin America and the Middle East where the movement is seeking new support.

This department, working on the basis of materials produced by the Research Department, coordinates the Urgent Action system and all campaigns and special actions. It coordinates and monitors activities included in the regular Action Calendar and allocates case sheets and other action materials to the sections and groups. It takes a particular interest in work with target sectors, including trade unions and the medical and legal professions; it advises AI professional groups on their work and it coordinates AI's activities in the area of military, economic and cultural relations.

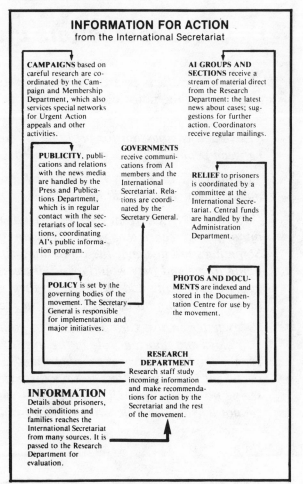

**INFORMATION FOR ACTION**
from the International Secretariat

**CAMPAIGNS** based on careful research are co-ordinated by the Campaign and Membership Department, which also services special networks for Urgent Action appeals and other activities.

**AI GROUPS AND SECTIONS** receive a stream of material direct from the Research Department: the latest news about cases; suggestions for further action. Coordinators receive regular mailings.

**PUBLICITY**, publications and relations with the news media are handled by the Press and Publications Department, which is in regular contact with the secretariats of local sections, coordinating AI's public information program.

**GOVERNMENTS** receive communications from AI members and the International Secretariat. Relations are coordinated by the Secretary General.

**RELIEF** to prisoners is coordinated by a committee at the International Secretariat. Central funds are handled by the Administration Department.

**POLICY** is set by the governing bodies of the movement. The Secretary General is responsible for implementation and major initiatives.

**PHOTOS AND DOCUMENTS** are indexed and stored in the Documentation Centre for use by the movement.

**RESEARCH DEPARTMENT** Research staff study incoming information and make recommendations for action by the Secretariat and the rest of the movement.

**INFORMATION** Details about prisoners, their conditions and families reaches the International Secretariat from many sources. It is passed to the Research Department for evaluation.

*Press and Publications Department.* This department handles all relations with the international news media and is responsible for the production and distribution of the *Amnesty International Newsletter*, leaflets and publicity material. It is in regular touch with section press officers and assists sections' publicity efforts. The work of the department also includes the development of new information materials, including audio-visuals, to enable AI to reach a wider and more international public.

In addition, the department is responsible for Amnesty International Publications (AIPs). This includes the editing, typesetting, designing, printing, selling and distributing of publications as well as their translation, revision and production in several languages. It is also responsible for liaison with *Unité francophone* (the publishing cooperative of the French-speaking sections) and the translation units of other sections.

The Press and Publications Department has two decentralized units outside London which provide information services in Latin America and Asia. One is in Colombo, Sri Lanka: the South Asia Publications Service (SAPS). The other is in San José, Costa Rica: *Publicaciones Amnistía Internacional* (PAI).

*Administration Department.* The Administration Department is responsible for all office management and financial procedures, including personnel, training and induction programs, accounts, travel arrangements and security. In consultation with the Treasurer, it prepares the annual international budget for submission to the International Council, administers the Relief Fund, and services the Financial Control Committee. It also maintains contact with section treasurers.

---

# *". . . your letters are of great value . . ."*

The following extracts are from a letter sent to an AI group by a former prisoner of conscience, imprisoned for the non-violent exercise of her human rights:

*"Love and compassion for prisoners of conscience is doing so much to create bonds between people . . .*

*"I would like to thank you and your friends with all my heart for what you did for me and what you are still doing for my friends in my country . . .*

*". . . not all letters from overseas friends reached me and my family, but it is important to realize that your letters are of great value even if they don't reach us. Sometimes in the camp, the camp authorities and warders would start to be especially polite to me and they would avoid ill-treating other women prisoners in my presence. I guessed something had put them on their guard. Later on just by accident I found out that a letter from abroad had come for me and caused this change in their behaviour.*

*"Any letter or post card addressed to political prisoners, their families or to officials . . . plays an important role in the lives of the prisoners. It improves their position even if the letters never reach their hands. So again and again I repeat: be patient and persistent in writing letters to save these people. Even if you get discouraged from seeing no results from all your efforts—what you write makes a difference . . . we cannot live and struggle without help from other democratic countries."*

# Chapter 6

# Fund-Raising and Finances

Financial independence is as vital to AI as its political independence.

A movement that started working in 1961 out of a small office where volunteers often paid for the postage from their own pockets, has grown into a permanent campaign needing a regular international budget.

Demands on the organization have grown as more and more prisoners have been arrested and as torture and executions have spread. Despite the increased costs of exposing and campaigning against these abuses, the movement has decided that it must rely on the efforts of its members and donations from the public.

This reliance on public support is essential to keep the movement free from interference by governments, funding agencies or pressure groups. It must remain independent, impartial and self-financing.

Financial guidelines ensure that all donations are made in accordance with the AI Statute and that no funds are received that would compromise the movement's integrity. No funds are received from governments for the international budget.

## Every donation makes a difference

Thousands of AI members and supporters give their time and money in an effort to end injustice. Every donation helps to build a broad popular movement, backed up by independent financial support, reflecting public opinion throughout the world.

Fund-raising is therefore a vital part of the work of everyone in the movement. Individual members pay membership fees and many give an additional contribution to help keep the work going. All groups organize their own fund-raising activities — collecting money on street corners, selling second-hand books, holding special events, organizing local concerts and art exhibitions and asking local personalities for donations.

AI sections also share in fund-raising efforts. In some countries they organize extensive "direct mail" campaigns, asking selected individuals throughout the country to support AI with a donation. In others, they arrange major publicity events, usually involving well-known performers, from which the proceeds (ticket sales, sound recordings and film and television rights) go to AI. Some sections sell posters, badges, stickers, key rings and other items.

The International Secretariat helps sections with their fund-raising efforts by making suggestions about publicity and by supplying facts and figures about AI's activities. For example, the cost of the total international operation can be broken down into small units that people can grasp easily — one case sheet or one minute (see box).

> **Professional artists and public relations experts often give free advice and practical help to AI. On the next two pages are fund-raising suggestions prepared for AI's 20th anniversary in 1981:** *"Give a minute to Amnesty International"* **and** *"Where there's hope there's life"*.

## Tips on fund-raising

- Don't be afraid to ask for money. It's vital to AI's work and every donation is a practical contribution to the cause. Asking for donations is one of the best ways of showing people that AI is exactly what it says it is — a voluntary movement relying on public support.

- Don't be afraid to keep asking for money! People who support AI's campaign for human rights realize that money is always needed. A good idea is to ask people to make out a "banker's order" or "standing order": regular contributions paid automatically every year from their bank accounts.

# Give a minute to Amnesty International

Thousands of peaceable men and women are in prison today because of their political or religious beliefs. Many are held without charge or trial. Many have been tortured.

The liberation of each of these victims is being carefully planned by a network of Amnesty International volunteers working all over the world to combat political imprisonment, torture and executions.

At the heart of this global operation is an international headquarters that collects and analyses reports of arrests, trials and secret detentions.

After a report has been verified by expert research staff, Amnesty International members are ready to publicize the case and campaign to restore the victim's human rights.

It is a lifesaving operation and every minute counts.

## In one minute

• an urgent cable can be sent to a government, calling for the immediate release of a prisoner of conscience
• an international news agency can be alerted to the case of a critically ill prisoner
• a special one-page appeal on behalf of a torture victim can be duplicated for international distribution
• a long-awaited detail about a political trial can be filled in on one of the thousands of index cards that keep the headquarter's prisoner records accurate and up-to-date
• a quick phone call can be placed to the United Nations in an effort to prevent a group of political refugees being sent back to a country where they would face torture and death

## Cost?

The international nerve centre for this unique operation runs on £16 a minute. That adds up.

And so does the cumulative effect of the research and appeals that have made Amnesty International one of the most effective voluntary movements for the defence of human rights.

Every minute's worth comes from donations by people who hate injustice.

---

£16 a minute for freedom means £1,996,800 a year. That's what Amnesty International will need this year to keep its lifelines open.

| | |
|---|---|
| A minute | £16 |
| An hour | £960 |
| A working day | £7,680 |
| A five-day week | £38,400 |
| A month | £153,600 |
| A year | £1,996,800 |

- - - - - - - - - - - - - - - - - - - ✂ - - - - - - - - - - - - - - - - - - - - -

Enclosed is the sum of _____
                                        (please print)

Donor's name _____
                                        (please print)

address _____

_____

_____

☐ Please send me a subscription to the *Amnesty International Newsletter* and *Report*.
☐ Please send me more information about the global campaign for human rights.

**Please give as much time as you can.**

Today thousands of peaceable men and women are in prison because of their political or religious beliefs. Many are held without charge or trial. Many have been tortured.

To bring the hope of freedom to all these people requires organised effort on a worldwide scale – a "conspiracy of hope", open to everyone prepared to work in defence of human dignity. That conspiracy is alive now, and has already proved effective. Its name is Amnesty International.

Amnesty International has supporters and groups in more than 130 countries throughout the world. It is independent of any national, ideological or religious grouping. It works for the release of prisoners of conscience everywhere, provided only that they have not used or advocated violence.

In less than 20 years Amnesty International groups have intervened on behalf of more than 20,000 prisoners in over a hundred countries with governments of widely differing political ideologies.

Countless prisoners remain. Many are held in remote labour camps or in distant island prisons. But nowhere is a prisoner beyond the reach of hope. And where there's hope, there's life:

"FAITH IN YOUR EFFORTS AND CONCERN SUSTAINED ME THROUGHOUT THE HORRIBLE PERIOD OF MY IMPRISONMENT WITHOUT HOPE I THINK I WOULD HAVE DIED"

PRISONER, PANAMA, NOW FREE.

"WHILE IN JAIL I HAD NO CONTACT WHATSOEVER WITH THE OUTSIDE WORLD. HOWEVER I REALIZED THAT THE ONLY WAY TO SAVE MY LIFE WAS TO ROUSE WORLD PUBLIC OPINION AND FERVENTLY HOPED THAT MY FRIENDS AND COLLEAGUES WERE TRYING TO DO SOMETHING ON MY BEHALF. MY HOPES WERE NOT IN VAIN. THANKS TO THE UNTIRING EFFORTS OF AMNESTY INTERNATIONAL AND MANY OTHER PUBLIC INSTITUTIONS & FRIENDS, VOICES OF PROTEST AGAINST MY TERRIBLE PLIGHT WERE RAISED ALL OVER THE WORLD"

PRISONER, BULGARIA, NOW FREE.

These are encouraging words, but we are under no illusion about the enormous challenge we still face. Our aim is to expand our international movement to the point where world public opinion will finally put an end to the nightmare of secret arrests, torture and killing.

The more supporters we have, the more we can do. If you would like to help, please fill in the form below. But first, if you have access to a duplicating machine, pass on this message: make six copies of this leaflet and send each to a friend who you believe would also be willing to help us bring the hope of freedom to the world's prisoners of conscience.

"I CAN NEVER FORGET HOW I WAS MOVED TO TEARS WHEN UNEXPECTEDLY I WAS HANDED IN A SOLITARY CELL A BRIEF LETTER FROM AMNESTY INTERNATIONAL"

PRISONER, TAIWAN, NOW FREE.

I wish to support the work which Amnesty International is doing to free prisoners of conscience and to stop torture and executions.

As a first step I am sending a donation to aid prisoners and their families and to increase the pressure on governments to respect human rights regardless of politics.

I enclose a money order for
Please make your donation payable to
AMNESTY INTERNATIONAL

NAME

ADDRESS
( PLEASE PRINT )

Please return this form to:

☐ Please send me further information about Amnesty International.

● Don't miss any chance of asking for a donation. Everyone who comes to an AI event or a group meeting should be asked for a contribution. Always encourage people to make a "silent contribution": paper money doesn't make a noise when it drops into the box.

● Don't forget to put the local or national AI address and bank account number on every leaflet and publication.

# AI's finances

AI's finances are controlled by the International Council and International Executive Committee. The Council establishes the movement's international budget and monitors its international financial procedures. The Treasurer, who is elected by the Council to the International Executive Committee, is responsible for the budget and supervises its expenditure. All sections are required to submit annual financial statements to the International Executive Committee. The audited accounts of the International Secretariat are submitted to the International Council.

The income for the international budget comes almost entirely from funds raised by AI groups and sections. Strict guidelines have been established by the International Council for the acceptance of such funds (reproduced in full in Chapter 11). Before accepting any money, whether directly or through sections, AI establishes that the contributions are in accordance with these guidelines which ensure that:

—AI is, remains, and is seen to remain independent and impartial;

—AI is and remains broadly based and self-supporting;

—AI's funds are given in accordance with the objectives of its Statute.

No government donations can be accepted by any part of the movement, nor can government money be sought for the international budget. Funds for relief work (as is usual in the case of humanitarian and charitable organizations) may be accepted from any source, including governments and their agencies, but all such funds must be administered under the exclusive control of AI.

The International Executive Committee must be notified of all donations to sections that amount to more than five per cent of their annual income. The committee then decides whether each such donation can be accepted in the light of these principles.

The funds are used for the services of the International Secretariat and to pay for international activities such as missions, international conferences, representation at the United Nations and on AI publications and publicity. The budget also covers the cost of maintaining communication throughout the organization and coordinating its international activities.

All AI sections pay a registration fee. The "fair share" each section is expected to contribute to the international budget is based on a formula which includes a "group-related fee" (according to the number of groups in the section) and an "income-related fee" (which is a percentage of the section's total income, as agreed by the International Council).

In addition to the international budget, AI has a relief fund and a Program Reserve and Special Projects Fund, contributions to which are received from sections, groups, members and supporters.

A Financial Control Committee comprising representatives from three sections or countries is elected by the International Council to supervise and undertake regular reviews of the financial administration of the International Secretariat to ensure that all necessary financial procedures are being followed.

# Chapter 7

# One Movement, One Voice

## International team work

AI consists of thousands upon thousands of people working together for the same cause. That is its great strength. Every AI member is part of a worldwide team. Each one is responsible for ensuring that AI continues to speak and be heard as one movement. Today's instant global communications make it all the more important that the movement's statements — whether made in Mexico, Sweden or Japan, or whether made by a local group or the International Secretariat —are based on the same accurate information and reflect the movement's common mandate and policy.

Each level of the movement, local, national and international, has elected or appointed officers responsible for issuing AI information to the public. For example, the press officers are responsible for all contacts with journalists — and the board of each section is responsible, after consultation with the International Secretariat, for approving any statement issued by AI in their country. These procedures are necessary to keep all public statements up-to-date, accurate and properly coordinated with other initiatives.

In 1979 the International Council decided that all section publications arising from research by a section should be approved by the International Executive Committee before publication. In practice, approval is now the responsibility of the Secretary General. This procedure was introduced to ensure that all AI information would be accurate and impartial. The International Secretariat procedure for checking and approving drafts of its own publications and news releases is used for section drafts. The following guidelines apply:

- AI's reports and public statements must conform to the organization's Statute and its international policy. The International Council has set strict limits on AI's mandate. These limits must be respected — AI does not report or comment on human rights abuses not within its terms of reference.

- AI's reports and public statements must be, and be seen to be, impartial. The organization does not support or oppose any government or political system. There must be no grounds for accusations that it takes sides in political conflicts.

- AI's reports and public statements must be accurate and precise. They must present facts about specific human rights violations and reports of such violations. They should *not* include partisan opinions or political speculation. AI does not comment on the possible reasons for human rights abuses or government motives.

- AI's reports and public statements must always make clear the nature of the source of allegations and any other information that has not been confirmed by the organization. Great care must be taken when republishing claims by other people or groups. Only if AI thinks there are grounds for believing that the information is reliable should it be cited. For this reason, much information given to AI cannot be published: it cannot be confirmed and cannot be reported as reliable. The reproduction of statements by others may often need to be prefaced with the warning "AI does not necessarily share the opinions or conclusions of the author".

- AI's reports and public statements must not give the impression that the organization supports the views of the prisoners whose rights it seeks to protect. AI is not a political support group and does not endorse any other cause.

- AI's reports and public statements must concentrate on the issues that fall within its mandate. Background information should not overshadow the description of matters of concern to AI or give the impression that AI is taking a stand on issues that are not within its mandate.

● AI's reports and public statements must be worded so as to be consistent with its policy of impartiality. For example:

(a) it does not label governments "regimes" or "dictatorships", or describe them or their leaders as "reactionary", "fanatical" or "despotic";

(b) it does not use vague labels when describing political parties, opposition movements or other organizations. It describes their policy and avoids interpretations;

(c) it does not use unnecessary adjectives and adverbs for extra effect. The facts themselves are usually sufficiently shocking: additional emphasis is unnecessary and can undermine AI's credibility as an impartial and reliable source of human rights information.

● Graphics, cartoons and photographs used in reports and public statements must conform to the same standards of accuracy and impartiality. They should be used because they are directly relevant.

AI compiles and circulates a lot of information. There are handy, easy-to-use documents that a well-informed AI member needs. Make sure you have access to them.

There is the *Amnesty International Statute*. Be sure it is the up-to-date text, including any changes made at the most recent meeting of the International Council.

The best account of recent AI work is the latest annual *Amnesty International Report*. This is also the basic reference document about AI's concerns around the world. When using an annual report, remember that it is a reference document covering a specific 12-month period and so cannot be completely up-to-date. Annual reports up to and including the 1981 edition cover the periods up to the end of April of each year; the 1982 edition covers the period to the end of 1981 and subsequent editions are planned to cover calendar years.

Any more recent information is contained in published country reports or external circulars, all of which are sent regularly to all sections. As well, the monthly *Amnesty International News-letter* is an easy-to-use source of up-to-date reports. Keeping a file of *Newsletters* is a good way of keeping abreast of all major AI concerns.

The *Weekly Update Service* sent from the IS to sections often contains information which is specifically supplied in order to help inform the news media about current problems. Much of the information in the *Weekly Update Service* and in circulars sent out each week is marked EXTERNAL. Be careful. Do not include information or advice marked INTERNAL in a public statement or give it to journalists. INTERNAL information is guidance and advice for AI members, often on organizational matters.

Much of AI's work is based on internationally recognized human rights standards. One basic document about them is the *International Bill of Human Rights*, which includes the *Universal Declaration of Human Rights* and the two human rights covenants. Other international agreements are the *Standard Minimum Rules for the Treatment of Prisoners* and the *Declaration on the Protection of all Persons from Torture.*

# Speaking to the news media

AI began with a newspaper story and the news media have played a vital role in helping the movement grow and be effective. At all levels of the movement AI needs to maintain a relationship of mutual respect and confidence with journalists. Responsibility for this rests with the press officers — in each group and section.

*The Press Officers.* All sections have a press officer responsible for coordinating media work in their countries and for all contacts with the national news organizations. Each section has its own procedures for communicating with the news media and for ensuring that group-level initiatives are carefully coordinated. Many sections have their own manuals for group press officers. The International Secretariat has prepared a general *Press Officers Manual*.

The press officers are always responsible for coordinating press contacts. If other AI members are given the opportunity to talk to the press, they must first consult their group or section press officer, thereby ensuring that there is one person who always knows what is being said to

THE OBSERVER WEEKEND REVIEW

# The Forgotten Prisoners

**The article that launched the AI campaign in 1961: "Open your newspaper any day of the week and you will find a report from somewhere in the world of someone being imprisoned, tortured or executed because his opinions or religion are unacceptable to his government. . . . The newspaper reader feels a sickening sense of impotence. Yet if these feelings of disgust all over the world could be united into common action, something effective could be done. . . . The important thing is to mobilize public opinion." The appeal attracted wide attention. Translations of the story appeared in the press in other countries ranging from France to India. Within months the groundwork was laid for a permanent international campaign.**

the press and can ensure consistency. Press officers can usually offer advice on how to handle interviews — they may know the reporter or the newspaper and will know what information has already been prepared for distribution to journalists.

The press officers answer most of the questions that come in from the press. This is by far the most effective and efficient procedure. They learn to recognize what reporters are looking for and what their problems, deadlines and procedures are. They can provide a service that hard-pressed professional journalists appreciate.

When a reporter wants a detailed interview about a particular prisoner or country and a country coordinator or other specialist is available, the press officer will usually ask that person to talk to the reporter.

Section press officers issue news releases to their national press after consultation with the International Secretariat Press Office, and

usually arrange distribution of international news releases (which come from the International Secretariat) to the press in their countries. Group press officers issue news releases to the local press. Groups should consult their section press officers for advice about the procedures in their countries.

*Basic Rules.* The three-way division of AI responsibility for press work matches the organization of the news media — local, national, international. As a result, the following rules should be observed:

- Group press officers should check with their section press officer before sending material to national publications or broadcasting stations. It can damage AI's work if editors of major organizations are bombarded with uncoordinated statements from groups.

- Do *not* send news material to the press outside your own country. You may be unintentionally conflicting with the work of AI members and staff in other sections or the International Secretariat. There are exceptional cases, usually special campaigns when members may be asked to write *letters* to foreign publications, but you should do this only when asked to by the International Secretariat. Any other exceptions must also be agreed in advance.

- If you are in an area where there are representatives of international news agencies or radio networks, remember that they are supplied with news and information by the International Secretariat, and are usually in regular contact with the International Secretariat Press Office.

*News releases.* The most common way of getting information to news outlets is the news release. Many group press officers receive advice from their section on how to prepare and issue news releases. The following general advice may be useful to groups if they have not received such guidelines:

- News should be presented in the way that editors require it. By writing a news release in the required style you can reduce the risk of having it rewritten and distorted.

● The first step in preparing any news release is to ask: how can the most important idea be presented in one clear sentence? If the public were to read or hear just that sentence would they have got the essential message?

● Journalists have a simple formula for telling the story in the first sentence. They ask, does it answer most of the questions: what, where, when, who and why? It is not always necessary or possible to answer all of those questions, but think about which are necessary for your news release.

● Be clear and straightforward. Be as brief as possible. A long, complicated news release will be thrown away or rewritten. The more it is rewritten, the greater the chance of your message being lost.

● Always say clearly who is issuing the news release. A local group may issue a release only in its own name and section news releases must clearly say, for example, "The Venezuelan Section of Amnesty International said today . . .". The only news releases which say "Amnesty International said today . . ." are those issued by the International Secretariat.

● Always include an explanation of what AI is and does, even if it is only a brief phrase such as "the worldwide human rights movement".

● Give the date at which any information or description was accurate. ("As of 15 May they had not been charged. . . .")

● In group news releases the news is often the activities of the group itself. The local press wants news of what is happening in its community and your news releases must take this into account.

● News releases should be typed, double-spaced.

● At the top of the news release the first thing the editor should see is who is issuing it: "Amnesty International Adoption Group 451, (town) and (country)"; then usually an address and, if possible, a telephone number and the name of the person to contact with questions.

    On a line by itself should be the embargo date and time — the clear instruction: "For Immediate Release Today Tuesday 1 June 1985".

● Next should come a short, simple headline.

● If you are aiming at radio stations, read your draft news release aloud. Could a news broadcaster use it without much change?

    A bad news release is often worse than none. If it confuses or fails to get your message across, contains errors, or makes editors think AI is a trivial organization, it can damage your work. A news release that only repeats back to the newspapers the human rights information they have already printed, without adding new facts or ideas, will not make them take AI seriously.

    If, however, you have a clear message and there is something new to say, you will have a good news release. Your new information may simply be what AI — or your group — is doing about a situation that is already known to many readers: holding a meeting or some other event. Don't be discouraged if a particular news release is not used by editors (but don't complain to them either). There are many pressures and problems which you may not know about which can squeeze out newsworthy items every day.

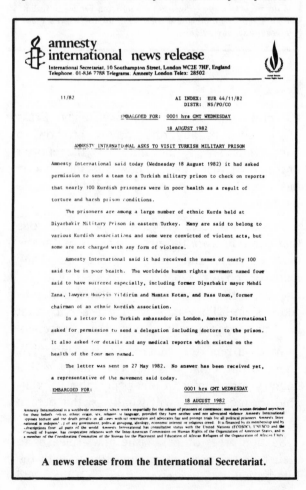

**A news release from the International Secretariat.**

# Publications

Over the years AI has developed an extensive publications program. AI information is now widely available in books, newsletters, leaflets, posters, films, tapes and slides.

Amnesty International Publications (AIPs) are issued under the authority of the International Executive Committee. They include the annual *Amnesty International Report*, the monthly *Amnesty International Newsletter*, reports of AI missions and other publications on countries or human rights themes. AI sections receive stocks of all these publications from the International Secretariat and groups may order them from their section. A publications catalogue is available from the International Secretariat.

The *Amnesty International Report* and the *Amnesty International Newsletter* are also available on subscription in three languages from the secretariat.

The annual report provides a country-by-country survey of AI's work to combat political imprisonment, torture and the death penalty throughout the world. The report is organized in regional sections and normally covers developments in at least 100 countries. This is probably the most widely read — and most influential — of the many reports published by AI each year.

The monthly newsletter provides a regular account of AI's work: the latest reports of fact-finding missions, details about the arrest and release of political prisoners, reliable reports of torture and executions. It also gives practical information for AI supporters: each issue includes appeals on behalf of prisoners of conscience and victims of torture and the death sentence around the world.

The newsletter is widely used by journalists, students, political leaders, medical doctors, lawyers, other professionals and human rights activists throughout the world.

AI sections also issue their own publications. If these concern countries and include material not already issued by the International Secretariat, the text must be approved by the Secretary General. The same procedure applies to group publications of this sort which must first go through the approval procedures in each section.

**Amnesty International**

*1982*

## publications catalogue

AI's reports get worldwide coverage in the news media and have a growing readership. Below, in one Asian country, students go through the reports in the "AI corner" set up in a local public library.

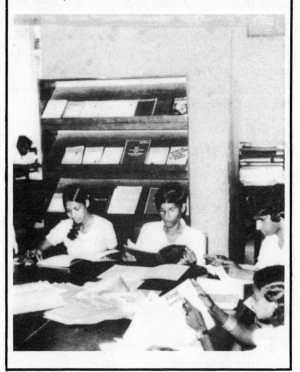

# An international personality

*"... an effective and popular movement of well-meaning, stubborn people who will not go away or shut up — backed by impartial, authoritative research ...".*

AI has an international personality. Any statement or activity by AI in one country can affect the perception of AI in other countries. Responsibility for maintaining AI's credibility and effectiveness rests with all parts of the movement — sections, groups and members. The movement depends on a thorough understanding by all its members of its principles and goals and on a spirit of international cooperation.

## International human rights

AI works for the protection of specific human rights that apply to all people. Social and cultural differences in the world do not invalidate these rights: they transcend the divisions of nationality, race, culture, religion and politics. These principles are the internationally recognized *human* rights that governments in all parts of the world have acknowledged and that are part of the heritage of the world's cultures. Even if legal codes and procedures vary from country to country and culture to culture, certain fundamental ideas remain common—the enduring values of justice, fairness, compassion and humanity.

## A specialized role

One thing more than any other gives AI its special character: its mandate.

AI is not concerned with all human rights, but is a human rights movement because it works in the field of human rights. To avoid confusion, AI members must always make clear exactly what AI does:

● it seeks the release of all prisoners of conscience
● it works for fair and prompt trials for all political prisoners

● it opposes torture and the death penalty for all prisoners without reservation.

AI in a single sentence:

"the worldwide movement that works for the release of prisoners of conscience, fair trials for political prisoners and an end to torture and executions".

## AI is impartial

AI's credibility stems from its impartiality.

The movement maintains a balance in its case work between different world ideologies and political groupings. It does not support or oppose governments or political systems. Nor does it necessarily support or oppose the views of the prisoners whose rights it seeks to protect. AI's exclusive emphasis on human rights — especially at a time when human rights issues are deeply politicized — is not always understood by governments and the public or by AI members. Nor is it understood by political groups that try to make use of AI and its information. Sometimes the fact that opposition groups use AI information in their campaigns may give the impression that AI itself offers a platform to such groups. But AI makes every effort to counteract this impression.

AI's impartiality also involves fair play with governments. It needs to be open with governments about the nature of the movement which combines both high-level diplomatic initiatives and grass roots campaigning. Governments need to understand that they can expect both sorts of approaches from AI.

## AI is accurate

AI is a movement that combines personal initiative by thousands of people with a need for strict accuracy in all its information and communications. Accuracy is not only a question of facts.

It is also a question of how information is presented, a question of style.

AI makes a distinction between allegations and facts. It lets the facts about human rights abuses speak for themselves. Every effort is made to specify AI's limited concerns in the field of human rights and to distinguish it from anti-government and political groups. The organization presents itself as somewhat anonymous: it is a collective institution with its own democratic and procedural checks and controls rather than a body that pushes forward personalities.

## AI is independent

AI must be and be seen to be independent — politically and financially. Political independence not only affects the need to make clear the impartial, non-partisan character of the work for human rights, but also the limits on cooperation with other organizations. AI does need to co-operate with other groups, but it must avoid having its independence and integrity compromised.

Financial independence remains a key factor in establishing the movement's credibility. Present practice excludes funding from national governments for section budgets and the international budget.

Local self-sufficiency is another element in demonstrating AI's financial independence. If AI is to be seen as an "international concern growing out of the local soil", the search for local funds must be part of that.

## AI is practical

The practical nature of AI's work must be clear in all publicity and recruiting material. This not only reinforces the non-partisan nature of AI's concern but also makes it clear that AI is seeking activist supporters.

The fact that the core of AI's activity is direct, personal work for other people is an important factor in mobilizing support from others.

## AI is effective

AI does not claim credit; it does not know all the factors that lead to the release of a prisoner of conscience. Experience inevitably leads AI to be modest when it compares its efforts with the scale of political imprisonment, torture and the death penalty throughout the world. Nevertheless, there is growing evidence that the letters and telegrams have some impact; they are not lost or callously brushed away by uncaring officialdom.

The wide variety of circumstances affecting individual prisoners and the considerable unevenness of AI's information in so many areas, makes statistical evidence of effectiveness unreliable and often misleading.

More convincing are the letters and statements from prisoners, from their families and colleagues and from former prisoners:

> "I can never forget how I was moved to tears when unexpectedly I was handed in a solitary cell a brief letter from Amnesty International."
> — a released prisoner of conscience

## AI cares

AI has to be careful and restrained, accurate and balanced in its statements, because it is trying to persuade powerful institutions to open their jails, close down their torture centres and dismantle their gallows. Human lives are at stake and care is needed if the right result is to be achieved. None of that caution means that AI is cold or unfeeling. Exactly the opposite. AI is a movement that cares deeply about people.

## AI is participatory

AI members participate directly in the work: they make the movement's policy, raise the money and carry AI's message to governments and the public. For the "lady next door", AI is the group member in her street. It is also the members who create AI's image with governments. Most high-level AI missions, in reporting back, have noted the impact that the thousands of letters had made on senior government officials. Each letter and their cumulative effect had spoken for AI and shaped the government's view of the movement.

## AI is constructive

AI is a watchdog, investigating and reporting human rights abuses, but the underlying purpose of its work is constructive. It is against imprisonment of people for their beliefs, because it is *for* the right to freedom of conscience without threat of arrest and detention. It is *for* freedom from torture. It is against cruel treatment and executions because it is *for* the dignity of the human person.

# Chapter 8

# General Advice on Action

The general advice and suggestions for action in this chapter apply to all aspects of AI's work. Case work is discussed more fully in Chapter 9.

The following items are relevant to all AI members:

- security
- coordination of activities
- relations with international organizations
- relations with exile and other organizations

Many of the subsequent items are relevant to AI sections or coordination groups and, wherever necessary, directions have been given on the need to consult the International Secretariat or your section.

No AI group is expected to undertake all the activities suggested in the following pages. Each group must plan its activities within the overall framework of its section. Chapter 9 outlines the particular responsibilities which each group is expected to fulfil in addition to those indicated in this chapter.

## Security

AI members are expected to treat information responsibly. Human beings may be placed at risk if sensitive information is not handled with discretion.

All circulars issued by the International Secretariat to sections, coordination groups or groups are marked either INTERNAL (for AI members only) or EXTERNAL (for general distribution).

INTERNAL documents are for circulation to AI members only. They must be carefully stored. They contain recommendations for action and information for members. Under no circumstances should INTERNAL documents be given to journalists, government officials or other organizations, sent to contacts within the country

concerned or given to people who are not AI members.

Letters from the International Secretariat, even if they do not contain confidential information, are themselves INTERNAL documents. They should not be circulated outside the membership.

EXTERNAL documents may be used by anyone. They contain important information for sections, groups, the public and other organizations. They may be reproduced, translated, and freely circulated.

Every prisoner dossier issued by the International Secretariat includes detailed security advice in the general instructions which should be observed by AI members. See Working Rule 56.

## Coordinating Activities

AI activities need teamwork. No one at any level of the movement works in isolation. The sensitive nature of the work makes proper communication and coordination vital.

AI sections and groups are required to send reports of their activities to the International Secretariat. The particular reporting requirements for groups are outlined in Chapter 9.

There are a number of Working Rules, included in Chapter 13 of the handbook. Most are designed to ensure proper communication and coordination between groups, sections, the International Secretariat and the International Executive Committee.

All AI members and workers are expected to consult their immediate colleagues when planning any activities so that they appropriate people (at the national and international levels) know about new projects well in advance, thus avoiding unnecessary confusion and ensuring the best use of information.

# Relations with International Organizations

AI groups and members sometimes want to seek help or advice from other international organizations. All letters to any international body must go through the International Secretariat. The secretariat is in regular contact with a wide range of other international organizations; to avoid confusion, groups should not write to them direct. Among the many international bodies to which this applies are: the United Nations, UNESCO and all United Nations agencies, regional bodies such as the Inter-American Commission on Human Rights of the Organization of American States, the International Committee of the Red Cross, the International Commission of Jurists, the International Association of Democratic Lawyers, the International Confederation of Free Trade Unions, the World Confederation of Labour, the International Labour Office, the International Federation of Journalists and the International Press Institute. A number of these organizations now redirect all AI group letters to the International Secretariat; therefore, all contact with them should go through the secretariat. See Chapter 12 and the Working Rule 17.

# Relations with other Organizations

Other organizations often support AI's activities. However, as an independent body with a narrow mandate AI must be careful about how it cooperates with other organizations, especially in any public or formal manner. The movement's impartiality and independence must be protected.

AI usually cooperates with other organizations only to the extent of exchanging information. It does not cooperate formally or publicly with other bodies. For example, it does not organize joint public meetings or send joint missions to countries. Any exceptions to this rule must be decided by a section's executive board or by the International Executive Committee. Such exceptions are not common and have usually involved collaboration on general human rights education programs or broad themes. As a matter of policy, AI does not hold demonstrations or news con-ferences and does not issue public statements or publications with other bodies.

It should always be explained to other organizations that AI's policy of not undertaking joint activities is in order to protect the independent nature of AI and does not reflect either approval or disapproval of their aims or policies.

AI may, of course, give external information to other organizations and may send speakers to their events (other than news conferences); but normally AI does not sign resolutions or endorse conclusions or recommendations jointly with any other organization, or organize joint public meetings or appeals.

AI's position on joint activities often needs to be explained to exile organizations or individual exiles and refugees as they often give AI valuable information and support its work and may, from time to time, ask AI to support their own demonstrations and appeals. Most can appreciate and accept AI's policy especially if it applies consistently to all other bodies.

In addition to respecting AI's general policy on relations with other organizations, particular care needs to be exercised in contacting or working with refugee or exile groups. They are frequently infiltrated by hostile informers. See Working Rule 18.

# What is Pressure?

AI protects and frees prisoners of conscience by continuous action on their behalf. These actions are effective because of the facts upon which they are based and the ideals that inspire them.

But this alone is not pressure.

Pressure comes from the fact that these actions never stop. Their influence continues to grow.

One letter to a Minister of Justice is not pressure.

A second letter is.

Two letters from one person every week create a little more pressure; two letters from a few people every day create still more.

This may be enough to tackle a simple problem. But it is not likely to be enough to free prisoners of conscience.

Pressure to free prisoners of conscience can involve all of the following:

— sending hundreds of postcards and letters to the foreign government;

— distributing leaflets at trade fairs;

— issuing special appeals signed by prominent individuals;

— publishing frequent reports on the human rights violations by the governments concerned.

Every group and section has to create this volume of pressure on behalf of the prisoners and groups of prisoners on whose behalf they are working. They must try every possible means of reminding governments of their obligation to protect the human rights of their citizens.

Pressure is not only a matter of quantity. A single statement by a leading figure can sometimes have as much effect as a petition. On the other hand a delegation of school children to an embassy may receive greater publicity. Each form of action has a particular effect; the combined result is pressure.

AI members have learned from experience that this pressure needs to be carefully planned and may have to be sustained for years. To do this requires imagination and great determination.

# Letters

Letter writing is the most basic of all AI activities. Advice on this technique in case work is in Chapter 9 and sample letters are in Chapter 10. A number of points should always be borne in mind whenever letters are sent to government officials:

— letters should be firm but courteous;

— use the correct form of address and a polite style (see Chapter 10);

— avoid comments that might be regarded as politically motivated. Many governments are sensitive to what they regard as "interference in the internal affairs of the state", and may be only too ready to dismiss AI as a political conspiracy;

— emphasize personal concern for the prisoner and the country's international reputation. Stress positive aspects — respect for the constitution and judicial process — so as to encourage a response;

— refer to the Universal Declaration of Human Rights or the International Covenant on Civil and Political Rights or the country's constitution, if appropriate;

— if it is safe to mention AI, briefly state its aims and point out its policy of independence and impartiality. (To describe AI you can write: "an independent, worldwide movement that works for the release of all prisoners of conscience, fair trials for political prisoners and the abolition of torture and the death penalty".) **Always make sure that it is safe to mention AI: the recommended actions indicate if it is not.**

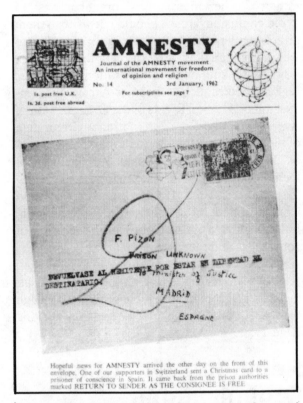

An early AI newsletter: the cover shows a postcard returned from prison to an AI member stamped, "return to sender as addressee is free".

# Appeals

Appeals can reinforce the impact of individual letters. There are at least four types of appeal you can use. As a general rule, an appeal should be launched after consultation with the section office.

**General Petitions.** A brief statement addressed to the head of state in question can be signed by thousands of people (giving their names, addresses and occupations) and formally presented to the ambassador for forwarding to the head of state.

**Appeals by Professional Category or Grouping.** A petition signed by people from the same profession as the prisoner, or from the same age group, religion or other category, can be an effective type of action.

**Appeals by Prominent People.** Try approaching prominent public figures for support. A statement signed by a number of outstanding people can have a significant impact on public opinion. The statement and the signatures can, with the signatories' permission, be sent to the authorities and simultaneously released to the news media in your country (through your section press officer). Appeals from individuals who are respected by, or sympathetic to, the government in question are likely to be especially influential.

**Appeals and Resolutions by Institutions.** Official statements by the governing bodies of universities, medical associations, and other institutions can have a great impact. Groups may approach several similar institutions in their country to make appeals on their prisoner's behalf. However, they must consult their section before doing so. See Working Rule 14.

# Delegations

A direct personal intercession on behalf of prisoners (visiting an embassy, for example) can be more useful than a letter of appeal, although such actions cannot have the sustained impact of a stream of letters and petitions. Both techniques must be used.

**Visits to embassies.** Many groups visit embassies regularly or arrange for other people to do so. This is always done in consultation with their section and country coordinator or co-ordination group. Embassy delegations should be small — about three people — and each person should be fully briefed on the case. It is a good idea for each person to raise specific questions: one person can ask about the prisoner's health, another about mail restrictions, another about legal difficulties, and so forth. It is important to have a request to make of the ambassador: Will s/he forward a letter to the government? Will s/he make inquiries about the prisoner? Such requests can be made at the end of the interview and will provide a basis for continuing discussion.

If the ambassador contradicts AI information, s/he should be asked to substantiate this denial — are there official reports available? Be firm about obtaining the facts.

Always consult your section office before planning such a delegation in order to avoid confusion and ensure the visit to the embassy would be in the prisoner's best interests (the section will consult the International Secretariat if necessary). Your section and the International Secretariat should get a report on each such visit.

A circular giving advice on embassy visits has been sent by the International Secretariat to all sections and may be consulted by AI groups in each country. Like other circulars it is available from your section or the International Secretariat.

**Delegations to visiting officials.** When representatives of other countries travel abroad make arrangements to meet them. This can be done through their embassies or trade commissions. Your section office must be consulted first to ensure proper coordination. A small group of AI members (perhaps with a distinguished person sympathetic to AI work) can meet the visitor, ask questions about his or her government's policy on human rights and why it has not replied to letters about prisoners. The visiting official may prove more helpful than the resident ambassador. Any failure on his or her part to keep a promise made to the delegation should be formally brought to the attention of the government concerned.
See Working Rule 14.

**Contacting elected representatives.** Writing to and visiting your elected representatives can be very helpful. You can ask them to write letters on behalf of the prisoners whose cases your group is working on. You can ask them to raise the case with your own government, especially if the question of providing asylum is involved. Try to arrange a meeting with your national, regional or local representatives, in consultation with your section and coordination group as appropriate. Take along the latest AI publications. Your group should make a specific request in any such meeting. For example, will the representative raise your group's cases with the Foreign Minister to see what further pressure can be applied for their release? Will he or she raise human rights questions when meeting representatives from other countries?

Records of these visits should be kept for future reference and copies sent to your section office. Follow up with letters and further visits.
See Working Rule 14.

# Public Actions

AI groups need public support. Every group has to get local publicity about its cases and campaigns. It needs people and community organizations to help circulate petitions, to respond to fund-raising appeals and carry AI's message to a wide audience. Most actions suggested in this handbook will help build this support; the following are aimed at reaching the general public.

Public actions require careful preparation. Some members of your group may already be familiar with these methods. AI section offices and experienced groups may also be able to give advice and help.

Assign responsibility for organizing the action to a working committee. Some people should be responsible for relations with outside guests or speakers, some for making arrangements if police permission is required and someone for dealing with the news media (press officer). Others may be responsible for placards and leaflets, or for fund-raising during the actions.

The committee as a whole should decide on policy such as the wording of placards, and relations with local authorities. If the committee anticipates any difficulties with the police, crowds, or hecklers, it should work out what its reactions and policy should be beforehand. This prevents petty arguments developing in the committee at a time when a unified response is needed.

Always bear in mind that AI must not act as a co-sponsor of a demonstration or public meeting with any other organization. See Working Rule 18.

**Films.** Organize a film show on political imprisonment. Follow with a short talk describing what AI is doing. Allow time for discussion and do not forget to take a collection. Suggest a follow-up to keep people involved. You can arrange a film show and discussion almost anywhere — in schools, churches, public meeting places or private homes. They are one of the best ways to raise funds, attract new members and arouse public interest.

**Public meetings.** Invite well-known individuals (journalists, writers, professors, members of parliament) to address a public meeting on an issue such as torture, political imprisonment or the death penalty. Arrange press coverage before and after. Particularly good speeches may be reproduced or quoted in leaflets, thus keeping the meeting "alive" long after it is over.

**Demonstrations.** Obtain permission from the police for a march to one or more embassies or to a public square. Always consult your section in advance. At an embassy, a delegation can deliver appeals or messages to the ambassador or, by appointment, discuss prisoner cases. Often AI groups with adopted prisoners in the same country join together to present a collective appeal on behalf of all adopted prisoners in that country.

Always think of the possibilities for mass media coverage: set up a mock prison cage, read out the names of the prisoners for radio and television. Consult your section press officer in advance.

Marches are a good way of drawing attention to the plight of prisoners. However, some groups do not do this lest they antagonize the community. Common sense must be used here as in all activities. When in doubt, consult your section.

AI's worldwide petition against torture.

amnesty
international

International Appeal
to the President of the General Assembly
of the United Nations

*No one shall be
subjected to torture
or to cruel, inhuman
or degrading treatment
or punishment.* ARTICLE 5.
UNIVERSAL DECLARATION OF
HUMAN RIGHTS

*We, the undersigned,*

*call upon the General Assembly of the United Nations*

*to outlaw*

*the torture of prisoners throughout the world.*

On the occasion of the twenty-fifth Anniversary of the Universal Declaration of Human Rights, we present this Appeal on behalf of more than one million signatories in eighty-five nations.

*signed at the International Conference for the Abolition of Torture*
*Paris 10 December 1973*

# Symbolic Actions

Prisoners of conscience can be seen as symbols of free thought and belief. Often their plight underlines the importance of the right to freedom of expression. The jailers and executioners symbolize the unlimited state power, physical brutality and repression.

Symbolic actions can be organized to express these forces operating in society today. Often this "living poetry" can succeed in rousing people when other, more conventional, efforts have failed.

Wearing badges, displaying banners, holding vigils and torchlight processions, holding art exhibitions, observing minutes of silence, arranging symbolic funerals or prayer meetings, are all ways of mobilizing people to campaign for human rights. With proper press coverage and the release of an eloquent public statement, symbolic actions can be extremely effective, even if they last only a short time.

# Performances

Plays and concerts are an excellent way of giving AI's work a high profile and building practical support.

Write to a performer who lives in the area and ask if he or she would give a concert for AI. Can the group meet him or her to discuss the idea?

Approach the manager of a local cinema. What films are going to be shown in the coming season? Can there be an AI benefit performance on an opening night?

Contact the directors of the local theatre. Will they put on a play by an imprisoned writer or a play about political imprisonment? Will they have a special performance in honour of prisoners of conscience?

Is there a local "street theatre" troupe in your area? Would they be interested in using AI material to perform a mime at street corners or in parks? Prepare leaflets for passers-by highlighting the cases on which your group is working. Take photographs of the event and write a short feature article on it for local magazines.

Poetry readings or readings from the works of imprisoned writers are often popular and can easily be linked to appeals for the release of prisoners of conscience.

# Target Sector Work

AI groups can use existing social institutions to build pressure for the international protection of human rights. Four examples are given below.

ALL SUCH APPROACHES AND ACTIVITIES SHOULD BE PROPERLY COORDINATED —

- if you are contacting a local organization, ask if their executive is already in touch with the AI section in your country;
- inform the section office of all contacts established;
- inform other AI groups in your own city or town. See Working Rule 14.

**Trade Unions.** Many trade unions have supported AI by circulating petitions, by passing resolutions, by inviting AI representatives to speak at their meetings and congresses and by making donations. The International Secretariat issues a regular *Trade Union Bulletin* containing information on workers and trade unionists in prison. Some sections publish similar bulletins.

Asking trade unions for help is usually quite simple. Write to the General Secretary of the local trades council and either arrange to visit one of their meetings to introduce AI or invite one of their representatives to your next group meeting. If you are responsible for the adoption of a trade unionist prisoner, this is essential.

AI groups can ask a trade union for:

**Action assistance:** The union can publish an appeal or circulate a petition on behalf of particular prisoners, or send delegates to support public actions or speak at AI meetings. Groups in small sections should make a point of coordinating these activities: it may be possible to get trade union support for a wide range of cases.

**Advice:** The union can give advice on trade union structures in your country and in others which may help you in your case work.

**Diplomatic intervention:** The union may be willing to make representations on behalf of individual prisoners with the ambassador of the country concerned. It may urge elected representatives in your country to take an interest in such cases. And it can ask unions in other countries to take similar initiatives. Remember to coordinate all such activities with your section office or coordination group.

**Finance:** The union may give money for relief, for telegrams or for AI's work in general. If you approach unions for donations, make sure that you are well briefed on AI policy and that you are not duplicating with similar requests from AI to the same union.

Even if your group is not dealing with the cases of imprisoned trade unionists, it is worthwhile exploring possibilities for local cooperation —by addressing trade union meetings, circulating AI materials, and requesting financial support or material assistance. Many unions, for example, operate their own low-cost printing presses and may be willing to print AI literature; many are prepared to distribute AI material to their members.

**Religious bodies.** Many religious bodies support AI and are of great help in campaigns and case work. Groups should make every effort to get the support of local religious leaders. If your group is responsible for the adoption of a victim of religious persecution, this is essential.

Ask for help with:

**Action assistance:** Special services can be held to mobilize support for prisoners of conscience. Congregations can circulate petitions and Urgent Action appeals; they can send dele-gates to public meetings organized by your group.

**Relief:** The congregation can contribute to special fund-raising programs to provide relief for adopted prisoners or support for AI's work in general.

**Diplomatic assistance:** The congregation may send delegations to meet foreign ambassadors; it can write to the home government; it can ask fellow congregations in other countries to act on behalf of particular prisoners.

**Publicity:** The congregation may circulate or reprint AI material for their members. It may be worthwhile preparing special materials suitable for sermons or religious publications. Congregations may be willing to let you use their own duplicating equipment, as well as other facilities.

**Educational institutions.** Schools, colleges and universities can do a lot to publicize AI's activities, broaden awareness of human rights issues and give practical help to AI's campaigns. Try these ideas:

**Organization and publicity:** Encourage AI membership in local schools, colleges and universities — many now have their own AI groups;
● send members of your group to speak at student societies or meetings;
● include university and college students, staff members, staff associations and student societies on your mailing list (if there is no group at the university or college);
● ask if you can use the student printing press to reduce costs for leaflets and publications.

**Pressure:** A local school, college or university group can:
● send letters to foreign governments signed by distinguished members of the university;
● circulate mass petitions on behalf of prisoners of conscience or as part of major AI campaigns for signature by staff and students;
● publicize the Prisoners of the Month cases in the student newspapers;
● organize "teach-ins" on human rights issues;
● organize demonstrations, public meetings and symbolic public actions on behalf of prisoners;
● hold a "Human Rights Week";
● give AI briefings to delegations from their college or university when they visit foreign countries and ask them to inquire on behalf of particular prisoners.

**Human rights education:** In some countries AI has developed ways of contributing to local and national education programs. Special materials for schools have been prepared and are used by teachers in a range of courses.

Your group can:

● contact sympathetic teachers, teachers unions or educational leaders to discuss the need for human rights education among young people to increase respect for fundamental freedoms. (A small kit could be prepared, to be sponsored or distributed by the educational authorities.);

● contact producers of television educational programs in your area, suggesting a series of programs on human rights and the work of AI;

● contact schools or educational authorities to discuss the circulation of leaflets and information in local schools, or possibilities for classroom talks about AI;

● encourage younger school children to help AI by painting greetings cards or sending postcards to prisoners.

**Political parties.** AI groups often contact political parties in the course of their work, particularly when adopted prisoners are members of political parties with connections abroad. Appeals from political leaders or parties should be encouraged, especially if they come from those sympathetic to the politics of the imprisoning government.

Some suggestions:

**Action:** Delegates from several political parties may be willing to present appeals and petitions to embassies. An appeal from leading members of political parties is often particularly influential. Prisoners' cases can be raised at party congresses and conferences and resolutions passed in support of general campaigns.

**Diplomatic assistance:** Political parties sometimes send high-level missions to other countries for talks with the government. Delegates should be asked to raise the cases of prisoners of conscience during their visit. Similarly, when other countries' leaders visit your country, try to brief politicians so that they can raise questions about human rights with them. You should also try to ensure that your own government is briefed about AI's concerns before foreign dignitaries visit your country.

**Information:** Politicians can keep you informed about trade and cultural agreements with other countries. They can keep you informed about forthcoming visits and exchanges and may know some of the people involved. They can also give you advice and information about countries your group is dealing with.

**Lobbying:** Contact your section office to find out how it organizes lobbying and whether there is someone on the board responsible for relations with your national government. He or she may have formed links with government and opposition parties, as well as with politicians willing to help AI on individual cases or various issues. In some sections there are parliamentary groups who can advise.

**Local work:**

● Local political parties can be asked to give a talk to AI groups about their policy on human rights issues. They may be prepared to support AI initiatives on behalf of prisoners of conscience. Keep these local parties informed about AI activities in the area and ask local political groups to keep you informed about their meetings — especially if matters of concern to AI might arise;

● Members of your group can ask to speak to the local branch of a political party. Ask the branch to subscribe to the AI *Newsletter* and publications.

AI deals with matters that concern politicians of all shades of opinion; all are likely, therefore, to lend the movement a sympathetic ear. But all AI members should be cautious lest certain political groups use AI for their own ends. Groups should therefore take care that they are seen to be non-partisan and guard AI's impartiality. A broad base of support for AI's objectives from political parties of all persuasions is essential if the movement is to have sustained credibility at home and abroad. Does every member of parliament in your country receive the *Amnesty International Newsletter*?

# Chapter 9

# Case Work

## Responsibilities of an AI Group

Every AI group takes on responsibilities when it is formed and recognized by its section (or by the International Secretariat in countries where there are no sections). Each group must work consistently on behalf of the individual prisoners whose cases are assigned to it and it must participate in campaigning, fund-raising and other activities. The group must also ensure that it takes no action that might in any way harm or endanger the prisoners or their families or that might damage AI's reputation and hinder its work.

**Security:** Groups are entrusted with the responsible handling of information they receive. Every prisoner dossier contains the following advice:

1. Please keep all information about prisoner cases in a secure place such as a locked filing cabinet.

2. If any prisoner dossier or its contents is lost or stolen, *immediately* inform both the section headquarters and the International Secretariat Campaign and Membership Department. Please explain in detail the circumstances under which the information was stolen and the steps taken to retrieve it.

3. Please do not give any prisoner dossier or its contents to any person who is not a member of the group. Do not photocopy the contents of this dossier for any person who is not a member of the group.

4. If you wish to give information to other persons, organizations or journalists, the material should be written out separately and strict care taken to prevent the misuse of confidential material.

5. Please observe closely the distinction between confidential and non-confidential information. Normally all confidential information is noted on the specific sheet for this purpose in the prisoner dossier. In general, confidential material should not be revealed to any person outside the group.

6. Please do not give out more information about the prisoner case than is necessary in each instance.

7. Please take care in working with and when giving or receiving information from political refugees or exile organizations. Their help can often be of benefit to your work, but you should remember that such groups are often infiltrated by hostile intelligence agents. Do not adopt their suggestions for action without prior consultation with the relevant coordinator or the Research Department.

See Working Rules 18, 56 and 58.

**Reporting:** Groups must report every six months on their activities via their section (or to the International Secretariat direct in countries where there are no AI sections). Each group is part of a team effort, and it is essential that the activities of all parts of the organization be properly coordinated. Even if groups have not received any positive replies to their approaches, the Research Department needs to know the detail of the activities undertaken both so that it can assess AI's profile on a country and on individual cases and so that it can suggest other activities or develop new approaches. Group reports can help the section, coordination group and the Research Department to evaluate AI strategies and techniques on different countries. A special form is provided either by the section or the International Secretariat for these regular reports.

As well as the six-monthly reports, groups must inform the Research Department immediately about any new developments in their cases and send copies of any government replies they have received to their letters. Even if the letters do not appear to contain any useful information, they can be important to the Research Department. Copies should also be sent to the section or relevant coordination group. In particular, the International Secretariat needs to have copies of all letters from prisoners and their families and any photographs of prisoners and prisons groups may receive. The Research Department will advise groups whether and in what ways such material can be made public or used in exhibitions illustrating AI's work. A central library of all audio-visual material is kept by the International Secretariat.

The Research Department will also send to the group any new information or material that is received by the International Secretariat.

# International Secretariat liaison with local AI groups

Local groups are usually in touch with the Executive Assistants in the Research Department. Groups may also have contacts with the Campaign and Membership Department, which is responsible for the allocation of cases, the maintenance of release records, and the provision of general guidance to groups, particularly groups in countries where there is no section.

The Research Department includes all available information on cases in the case sheet, and will *automatically* inform groups if further information is obtained. There is therefore no need for groups to write to the Research Department to request further information. If groups do have a problem or query relating to a particular case, or would like suggestions for further action, they should first approach the relevant coordination group or their section headquarters. If these are unable to help, the matter will be referred to the relevant department at the International Secretariat. All inquiries about individual prisoners or countries will be directed to the Research Department. The Research Department is responsible for preparing case sheets, background papers and general campaign documents. The Executive Assistants, who work closely with researchers on particular countries or regions, are responsible for most of the correspondence between the Research Department and groups.

Letters to the International Secretariat should be addressed to the relevant department and CLEARLY MARKED WITH THE GROUP'S NUMBER AND THE NAME AND COUNTRY OF THE PRISONER CONCERNED — this will help to avoid delay. If groups are not sure which department to write to, they should contact their section headquarters. Where an urgent response is needed, this should be clearly indicated in the letter.

Although English, French and Spanish are the three official languages of the organization, staff are recruited internationally and English is the working language of the International Secretariat. Groups should, wherever possible, send letters and reports to the Research Department in English; materials in French and Spanish will often need to be sent for translation and therefore be delayed.

Copies of all letters from the International Secretariat to local groups are sent automatically to the section and coordination group for their information.

Although work on an individual case may be delegated by a group to a sub-group or to an individual member, the International Secretariat will usually send information and correspondence to the official address of the group which is sent to the secretariat by the section headquarters. Changes of address should be notified to the section and the relevant coordination groups immediately. The group's address should be as permanent as possible in order to avoid delays or confusion.

# Coordination

The address of the coordinator or coordination group in your section responsible for dealing with activities on behalf of prisoners in a particular country is included in the prisoner dossier. Copies of all correspondence from the International Secretariat to each group are sent to the relevant coordination group in the section. If groups have any inquiries or need further suggestions for activities, they should always contact the coordinator or coordination group in the first instance. Groups should write directly to the International Secretariat only if there is no appropriate coordinator or coordination group in their section.

**Every AI group receives a dossier on each case allocated to it.**

# Selection of Prisoner Cases

The Research Department is responsible for obtaining information about prisoners and for preparing prisoner dossiers for allocation to AI groups. It seeks to ensure that all information is properly verified before recommending any action. Following general guidelines such as the definition in the Statute of the term "prisoner of conscience", each case is evaluated on its own merits. The prisoner dossier explains in each instance why AI is taking action on the case. The prisoner dossier also indicates the "status" of the case which will be one of the following:

### Adoption cases

AI *adopts* detained individuals when it believes that they are PRISONERS OF CON-SCIENCE — men and women detained for their beliefs, colour, language, ethnic origin, sex or religion, who have not used or advocated violence. The reasons for adoption in each case are included in the prisoner dossier. Since the detention of a prisoner of conscience is in itself a violation of the Universal Declaration of Human Rights, AI works for the prisoner's immediate and unconditional release.

### Investigation cases

There are two different kinds of investigation case. In the first category, AI *investigates* the cases of detained individuals when it believes that they are likely to be PRISONERS OF CONSCIENCE, but where more information is needed to be sure of this. Groups will be asked to try to obtain this further information. In their inquiries to governments and in all other correspondence groups must make it clear that they are not appealing for the release of the prisoner but are seeking further information. When the case sheet recommends that the case be publicized, any public statements should indicate that AI is investigating the case only.

At a later stage, if sufficient information is obtained to ascertain that the person is a prisoner of conscience or if no satisfactory information is provided by the government concerned to indicate otherwise, the Research Department may decide, on the basis of all available information, that the case should be changed to an adoption case. It should be noted that the International Council has decided that "the assertion by a government that a political prisoner has used or advocated violence should not be binding on AI." If further information indicates that the detained person is not a prisoner of conscience, the case would be closed by the International Secretariat.

Sometimes it may not be possible to obtain any further information about a case and the possibilities for group action may remain limited. The Research Department may decide to review these cases where there have been no developments after a reasonable period (such as two years) and to suspend investigation work. The Research Department then continues to monitor the cases directly itself.

In the second category of *investigation* case, AI takes up the cases of political prisoners (who may not be eligible for adoption) who have been detained for long periods without trial or sentenced on the basis of unfair trial procedures. This policy is based on AI's opposition under Article 1b) of its Statute to the "detention of any prisoner of conscience or any political prisoner without trial within a reasonable time or any trial procedures relating to such prisoners that do not conform to internationally recognized norms."

In these cases the group is expected to protest to the authorities and call for the prisoner to be brought to trial. Investigation cases in this category may not be eligible for adoption and therefore the status of the case will remain investigation. Clear instructions will always be given in the prisoner dossier for activities to be undertaken by groups.

## Double and Triple Adoptions

In some adoption cases, two or three groups work on behalf of one case where this is felt to be in the interests of the prisoner. This is called "double adoption" or "triple adoption". When more than one group is involved, the names and addresses of all groups working on the particular case are included in the prisoner dossier. Each group should keep the other group or groups informed of its activities so that efforts can be coordinated and ideas and experiences shared. Groups may be asked to make it clear that they are one of several working on the case when writing to the prisoner, the prisoner's family or to contacts. Sometimes only one of the adopting groups will be asked to write to the family or other sensitive contacts. Instructions will be included in the prisoner dossier, as appropriate.

## Group cases

AI may take up the cases of several prisoners at the same time (or a whole prison) and treat this as a single case. This may be done, for example, if it is thought unsafe to adopt or investigate the cases of individual prisoners or if it is believed that action on behalf of all the prisoners will be a more effective technique to secure their protection or release. Full details on such cases and the work to be undertaken on their behalf are included in the prisoner dossier.

## "Disappearances"

People who are abducted for political reasons and "disappear" are the victims of arbitrary arrest and detention; many may face torture and death. The authorities do not even acknowledge their arrest. It is usually extremely difficult to establish their whereabouts and, often, to know whether they are still alive.

In such cases groups are advised to urge the authorities to make inquiries as to the prisoner's whereabouts or, depending on the circumstances, to acknowledge the arrest. AI normally treats "disappearances" as investigation cases until more information is received. Once the individual's detention is acknowledged or AI receives information that the person is in custody, the International Secretariat reviews the case to establish whether it should have adoption or investigation status.

## Prisoner Dossiers

Every group receives a prisoner dossier for each case assigned to it. The file contains the following:

— case sheet
— explanatory note on "Status of Case"
— general instructions leaflet
— recommended case action
— list of government authorities
— background materials

and where appropriate:

— confidential information sheet
— relief action
— guidelines for double and triple adoptions.

The *case sheet* contains any available personal details about the prisoner (age, profession, relatives, state of health); facts about the arrest, charge, trial and sentence and about the place and conditions of imprisonment. It provides a brief background to the arrest of the prisoner and details about the political or other circumstances.

The *"status of case"* explains the distinction between an adoption and investigation case and the action to be taken for each. It also describes group cases and "disappearances".

The *general instructions leaflet* lists the kinds of action which groups can take on behalf of prisoners. It gives advice on security, coordination and reporting and general guidelines on activities.

The *recommended case action* sheet gives specific instructions for action on the particular case. *These instructions take precedence over the general instructions and may prohibit groups from undertaking actions suggested either in this handbook or in the general instructions booklet.*

The *confidential information* sheet is included only where necessary and may contain advice or sensitive information such as the address of the family. *This information is not for publication or circulation*; it is not to be mentioned in letters to government officials or released to the press or given to anyone who is not a member of the group.

The *relief action* sheet is not always included in the prisoner dossier as it is quite usual for the relief needs of the prisoner and the family to become known only after the group has started making it inquiries.

The *guidelines for double and triple adoption* are included in any prisoner dossier assigned to more than one group. They provide advice about how groups should cooperate together.

All prisoner dossiers give a brief account of the political situation in the country concerned and of the laws under which the prisoner is detained. In many cases the Research Department provides a detailed background paper on the country or on a particular group of prisoners. Suggestions for further reading are often given. Group members should make every effort to familiarize themselves not only with the information provided by the International Secretariat, the coordination group and the section, but also with the history and culture of the countries concerned so that they are able to write informed and therefore more effective letters.

The amount of information reaching the International Secretariat about individual prisoners varies considerably. In some cases, such as those of well known politicians or writers, full biographical details will be available. In other cases an AI mission may have visited the country and observed their trial. More often, however, very little is known about the prisoner; he or she may be held incommunicado in an isolated prison. Groups should try to obtain fuller information in accordance with the suggestions in the prisoner dossier.

The Research Department includes in each case sheet all available information on the case. It also informs all relevant groups if it obtains further information about prisoner cases. Groups do not therefore have to write to the International Secretariat for more information; if it is available, it will be sent to groups automatically. The groups themselves should immediately pass on any news they receive in the course of their work. Such information may affect not only the prisoners they are working for

but others held in the same circumstances. It may not seem an important detail in itself but it will contribute to the accumulated information in the Research Department.

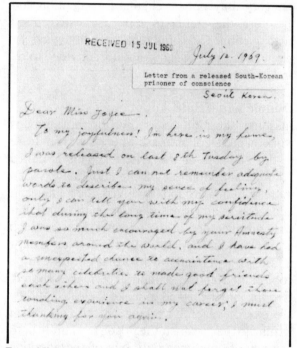

From AI's archives—a letter from a released prisoner of conscience. The letter states: "To my joyfulness! I'm here in my home. I was released on last 8th Tuesday by parole. Just I cannot remember adequate words to describe my sense of feeling, only I can tell you with my confidence that during the long time of my servitude I was so much encouraged by your Amnesty International members around the world, and I have had an unexpected chance to [make] acquaintance with so many celebrities to make good friends each other- and I shall not forget those touching experiences in my career; I must thanking for you again."

# Closure of cases

Once a prisoner dossier has been assigned to a group, the group must work on behalf of the case until the prisoner is released or the case is closed by the International Secretariat.

If a prisoner is released and there is no need for further action, the Research Department will notify the group on special "Closure of Case" notepaper. This is the official confirmation of the closure of the case. If there is a possibility that the prisoner may be arrested again the case will be closed but the group will be asked to keep the prisoner dossier. If this is not likely, the group will receive instructions from its section headquarters or coordination group (or from the

International Secretariat in countries without a section) about what to do with the prisoner dossier. The material contained in a prisoner dossier is confidential and must be handled with care. The group will therefore be advised to destroy the dossier or return it to the section for the section archives.

In cases where the prisoner is released from prison but is then sent into internal exile, served with a banning order, or faces trial, the group will be informed of the prisoner's change of circumstances but will be expected to continue working on behalf of the prisoner, as an adoption or investigation case.

Once a case has been closed by the International Secretariat, the group can apply to its section for another prisoner dossier or to the International Secretariat in countries where the section has not yet taken over responsibility for case allocation or where no section exists.

# Aftercare

In some cases, after a prisoner is released, there is still a need for assistance from an AI group. The Research Department will decide whether such assistance is appropriate and will change the status of the case from one of adoption or investigation to one of *aftercare*. The group will be asked to continue specified activities. Aftercare activities focus on humanitarian aid to the prisoner, for example, sending relief payments and keeping up correspondence with the prisoner and his or her family.

The duration of aftercare work is fixed at six months, although the International Secretariat may recommend that this period be extended or shortened if circumstances make this necessary and appropriate.

While a group is working on an aftercare case, it should submit six-monthly reports to its section, coordination group and the International Secretariat. If there is any new information about the person's situation, this information should be checked with the Research Department before any action is taken. Groups should also continue to send the Research Department copies of any correspondence received from the family or the released prisoner.

# Correspondence with government authorities

Care should be taken to ensure that letters reach the most appropriate officials and that the style, language and content are effective. Detailed advice on letter writing and sample letters are given in Chapter 10.

The prisoner dossier provides instructions for letter writing, as well as a list of the names and addresses of individuals or government authorities to whom groups should write. Instructions will be given as to whether letters should be written on AI stationery or from private addresses and which language should be used. Letters to the authorities in their own language or the main second language of the country may be most effective. Advice on this point is given in the Recommended Case Action in the prisoner dossier.

Letters should be written to a wide spectrum of officials. Extensive lists of addresses and names of officials are provided by the International Secretariat.

Groups can also send letters to ambassadors in their own country: these contacts can often enable a group to keep up a constant correspondence with the government.

Letters should be sent to governments regularly to sustain the pressure: for example, when the group receives a new case or further news about a prisoner, when a partial amnesty has been announced, on Human Rights Day (10 December), during AI's Prisoners of Conscience Week every year, on national holidays and religious festivals, on the President's birthday, and so on. Some groups write as often as once a week; all members of the group should try to write once a month. Follow-up letters should be written if replies are not received after a reasonable time.

It is important to exert pressure from every quarter, and therefore, in addition to letters from group members, the group should involve friends and important local personalities in writing in their own names to the authorities. Local organizations (such as trade unions, social institutions and professional associations) should be asked to appeal to the relevant authorities. The groups should provide addresses and details of the case as well as particularly important dates for appeals.

Many groups never receive replies to their letters — either from the foreign government or from the prisoner. Although this can be discouraging and frustrating, it is not a sign that letters are ineffective. Groups must keep on writing: it is an essential part of the constant collective pressure. Letter writing must be a regular and continuous activity, so that governments receive constant reminders that the prisoners are not forgotten and that there is international concern about their situation.

It is important not to abuse the foreign government or to use political jargon in letters. Letters should always be moderate and reasonable in tone; offensive language may result in harm to the prisoner. Letters should not include subjective judgments on the situation in the prisoner's country. It is better to write well informed letters which relate to the public image of the government internally and internationally. Many governments are anxious to appear fair and reasonable. It is important, if possible, to stress a country's reputation for justice, and to show respect for its constitution and judicial procedures. Reference should be made to human rights conventions and international standards which the government has ratified; details will be provided in the prisoner dossier.

There have been striking examples of the cumulative effect of letter writing in securing the release of prisoners even though the letters were never acknowledged.

Letter writing advice and sample letters are included in Chapters 8 and 10.

# Correspondence and meetings with government representatives

Groups should write to the local embassy, high commission or other representative of the prisoner's government accredited to their own country. General guidelines for this are given in Chapter 8. Reference can be made where appropriate to trading, cultural and diplomatic links between the two countries. Groups are more likely to receive a reply from an embassy than from its government and should, therefore, be persistent in writing letters.

These contacts may provide a useful opportunity to arrange an AI deputation to an embassy. Groups should always consult with their coordination group and section office first. These deputations are often most effective when they are organized nationally, involving representations on behalf of a number of AI groups with prisoners in the same country. Groups should also inform the Research Department of plans to visit an embassy.

Contact should also be made with embassies on the occasion of visits from government officials, or to coincide with international cultural events, after consultation with the coordination group or section.

Groups should bear in mind that AI does not support or oppose boycotts of any kind but may use a wide range of opportunities to raise its concerns with the relevant government and to raise public awareness about human rights issues.

# Publicity and Press Relations

One of the main tools for exerting pressure on behalf of prisoners of conscience is the use of publicity. Usually, groups are asked to publicize the cases they are working on, but groups must remember that there are cases where a lot can be accomplished by discreet efforts and that some types of publicity may antagonize a government. Sometimes the prisoner dossier will carry a warning not to publicize a prisoner's case: it may be that publicity would endanger him or her. It is usually possible to publicize the cases of adopted prisoners of conscience; with investigation cases, groups may be asked to avoid publicity until

An AI stall at a local fair. Groups publicize their cases and get public support.

further information has been obtained. But if publicity is recommended, groups should make every effort to carry out a sustained campaign on the prisoner's behalf.

A Press Officers Manual has been sent by the International Secretariat to all sections and press officers and may be helpful to local groups. The basic advice on publicity is contained in Chapter 7 of this handbook.

Prepare a short article on the work of your group and highlight the prisoner case. Always give readers an address to which appeals can be sent on behalf of the prisoner and include your group's telephone number or address. Many areas now have local radio and television stations which are willing to report activities taking place in the locality. Invite them to the public events your group organizes and talk to them about the cases you are working on.

Use every possible event to get publicity: national days, official birthdays, religious festivals, as well as the prisoner's birthday or anniversary of the trial. This is a systematic way in which to build up the cumulative pressure of publicity on the prisoner's behalf. Try to persuade influential people living or working in your neighbourhood to support your campaigns, remembering that appeals from people who sympathize with the government will carry greater weight with it than those from people who are known to oppose it.

The publicity campaign should be sustained: ensure that copies of publicity which you obtain in the media are sent to the relevant authorities. Send copies of the news clippings to ambassadors for their comment and to the appropriate officials of the country concerned.

See the Working Rules for general guidelines on publicity activity.

# Approaches to other organizations and institutions

General guidelines for approaching other organizations and institutions are given in Chapter 8. Many prisoners have a trade or profession and sometimes these are represented by national or international organizations (for instance, steelworkers, schoolteachers, journalists, agricultural

A Buddhist monk, member of a local AI group, talks to a meeting of students during Prisoners of Conscience Week. Groups help carry AI's campaigns to an ever growing public.

workers). Groups should contact the appropriate national body in their own countries and try to involve it in protests against the imprisonment of the individuals concerned. Sometimes the organization can put the group in touch with its branch in the prisoner's country or make inquiries on the prisoner's behalf. These approaches should only be made after consulting the relevant coordination groups and the section office. Chapter 8 gives clear guidelines on relations with international organizations and relations with exile bodies. All groups should follow these guidelines carefully. See the Working Rules.

# Correspondence with AI contacts

Names of contacts in the prisoner's country or elsewhere who might be able to provide information about the prisoner, the trial or the family, may be given in the prisoner dossier. Specific instructions will be given about how to write to them and these should always be followed strictly in the interests of the contact's safety and the safety of the prisoner and family. Groups are advised not to set about developing contacts themselves without prior consultation with the Research Department as this could seriously endanger the contact and may have a very negative effect on AI's work on that country or for that prisoner.

# Correspondence with the prisoner and family

Prisoners usually welcome letters from groups, but the extent to which prisoners are allowed to receive letters varies considerably. In some countries, prisoners are not allowed to receive letters at all; in others, the number of letters they can receive may be restricted. In some cases, the place of detention may not even be known to AI.

The prisoner dossier states whether it is possible to write to the prisoner. When in doubt, groups should contact the appropriate coordination group or the Research Department.

The prisoner dossier will also give the name and address of the prisoner's family where these are known and advice about how to contact them.

# Relief

Relief assistance can give material and moral support to prisoners and their families. It may pay for children's school fees, help to supplement an inadequate prison diet, pay fares to visit a prisoner, or buy medicine. After prisoners have been released, relief funds can be used for their rehabilitation. However, it is not always possible or advisable to send relief to prisoners and their families. The Research Department will give advice about any possible relief activities in the "Relief Action" sheet included in the prisoner dossier. Groups should under no circumstances undertake any relief operations other than those recommended in the prisoner dossier.

The International Secretariat distributes relief from central funds for large-scale projects and to individual prisoners and families. The prisoner dossier will advise groups whether there is a central channel for relief to the prisoners and their families. When sending relief money for distribution by the International Secretariat, groups should always state the name, address and number of the group and the name and country of the prisoner and project for whom it is destined.

When it is possible to send relief, advice about what to send and how to send it will be given in the prisoner dossier. For example, it may be better to send money rather than parcels. Groups may also, in some sections, be able to apply to the section headquarters for relief funds when they themselves have insufficient resources.

Groups should be sensitive to differences between cultures and be sure that relief items will be useful and acceptable before sending them; receiving large sums of money could be embarrassing to families in poor neighbourhoods. It is also important to remember that prisoners or families should not become dependent on external support to maintain their standard of living.

All details on the sending of relief are *strictly confidential* and for use within AI only. Government authorities frequently disapprove of efforts to send relief to prisoners or their families. Groups should *never* publicize the recipients of relief, the amounts sent to them or the channels used or disclose this information to anyone who is not directly involved.

The International Secretariat requires a regular report on all relief money distributed by each group.

# Visits to the prisoner's country

Sometimes it may be possible for group members who, in the course of business or pleasure, travel to countries where they have adopted prisoners to meet prisoner's relatives and even visit the prisoner. Group members who wish to visit these countries should consult the Research Department to find out whether such visits would be possible. After receiving the advice of the Research Department, the group should write to the family. No family should be visited without its express consent in advance, since a sudden visit from a foreigner could attract unwelcome attention.

Members on these visits are not permitted to speak or negotiate on behalf of AI. Such visits are quite separate from official AI missions which are authorized by the International Executive Committee only. See the Working Rules.

# Chapter 10

# Letters and Telegrams

Writing letters and telegrams is not difficult. They need not be long. You do not have to discuss complex political questions. All you have to do is show your concern about prisoners and make a simple request. Of course, anyone who wants to write longer or more sophisticated letters is welcome to. Many sections produce detailed letter writing guides, but the following basic advice may be helpful.

## Addresses

AI always tells you to whom each appeal should be sent. This can vary from a few names and addresses when a quick reaction is needed, as in an Urgent Action, to a long list of government ministers and other officials for long-term case work.

If, however, you cannot afford to write many letters abroad there may be an alternative. If the country concerned has a diplomatic mission in your country you can send the letter care of the embassy in the hope that it will be forwarded (as it should be). Addresses of high commissions, embassies and consulates are found in the telephone directory. Most AI sections can supply them.

## Opening and closing your letter

There are few universal rules on addressing officials. Practice varies from place to place. The most important thing is that your letter be polite and respectful. The following suggestions may be helpful as a general guide, but please follow the specific instructions in any case sheet or recommended actions if they differ from these.

Kings and Queens and other monarchs may be addressed as "Your Majesty".

Other heads of state, such as Presidents, may be addressed as "Your Excellency".

Prime Ministers and government ministers may be addressed as "Dear Sir", "Dear Madam", or as "Dear Prime Minister".

Ambassadors should always be addressed as "Your Excellency". High Commissioners (the term used for the representative of one country to another within the Commonwealth of Nations) should also be addressed as "Your Excellency". On the envelope you should write "His/Her Excellency the Ambassador for . . ." or "His/Her Excellency the High Commissioner for . . .".

However, only diplomats of ambassadorial rank are entitled to this title, and all other diplomats (including Chargé d'Affaires, Counsellor, First Secretary, Second Secretary, Consul, and so on) should be addressed as "Dear Secretary" or "Dear Consul" and so forth.

You can end your letter with the simple "Yours truly" or "Yours sincerely". However, many people prefer to be slightly more formal and write "Yours respectfully and sincerely".

> *"We could always tell when international protests were taking place . . . the food rations increased and the beatings inside the prisons were fewer . . . letters from abroad were translated and passed around from cell to cell . . . but when the letters stopped, the dirty food and the repression started again."*
> **From the statement of a released prisoner of conscience**

## Letters in your language

By all means write in your own language. If there is a local embassy there is no problem — send the letter to the embassy. Most embassies have staff capable of translating local correspondence. If the country has no embassy, then it may be possible to get a friend to translate the letter for you. But be sure to send both the original and the translation to the foreign government. (The translation should be headed "Translation from the Urdu", or Finnish, or whatever the language is.) Prisoner dossiers advise groups on the best language to use in their letters, but if you cannot get anyone to do a *good* translation for you, then write clearly and simply in your own language.

# What to say

Here is some general advice:

1. Always be polite. Your aim is to help the prisoner. Governments don't respond positively to abusive letters.

2. Write on the assumption that the government is open to reason and discussion.

3. If possible show respect for the country's constitution and judicial procedures, and an understanding of its current difficulties.

4. Follow the instructions given by AI in each case. For instance, if the *Newsletter* or Urgent Action appeal asks you to urge that a group of detainees get proper medical treatment, make sure that you request this, and not their trial or release which might be appropriate in other cases.

5. Never use political jargon. Stress the fact that your concern for human rights is not politically partisan but in line with the basic principles of international law.

6. It is preferable to give an indication of who and what you are. Some of the following sample letters do this. This shows that the letter is genuine and that people from various walks of life are following events in the country concerned.

7. If you have any special interests in or links with the country, it is a good idea to mention this in your letter. For instance, you may have visited it or studied its history.

8. A simple letter is adequate and is certainly better than no letter at all. But sample letters C and D might be considered the standard length when you have nothing special to add. A good rule is not to write more than one page (that is, one side). Only occasionally are long letters likely to be effective.

# Sample letters and telegrams

The following are examples only.

## SAMPLE LETTER A

Your Excellency,

I appeal for the release of ..............., a prisoner of conscience who has been held in Ngaragba Prison for the last three years. I urge you to take a personal interest in this case and ensure that he/she is allowed to rejoin his/her family.

Yours truly,

## SAMPLE LETTER B

Your Excellency,

I am writing to ask for the immediate and unconditional release of ............, who I believe has been imprisoned for the non-violent exercise of her right to freedom of expression in violation of the Universal Declaration of Human Rights.

Yours sincerely,

## SAMPLE LETTER C

Dear Prime Minister,

I am a teacher and a member of Amnesty International. I am concerned about the plight of ............ who has been detained for nearly three years under the Internal Security Act. No reason has been given for her detention.

Her imprisonment violates Article 9 of the Universal Declaration of Human Rights which states: "No one shall be subjected to arbitrary arrest, detention or exile." I therefore urge you to look into this case urgently and to order the release of ............

Yours sincerely,

## SAMPLE LETTER D

Dear Consul,

I am writing to you on behalf of ................. Although I do not know him personally, I am disturbed that he has been arrested and detained without any charge or trial. Everyone has the right to know the charges against them and to be presumed innocent until proved guilty. These fundamental human rights transcend the boundaries of nation, race and belief.

Your government has publicly stated that it seeks respect for universal human rights and your country has had high judicial standards. I therefore urge you to convey to your government my plea that ............ be charged under the law and given a trial that conforms to international human rights standards or be released without delay.

Yours respectfully and sincerely,

## SAMPLE LETTER E

Your Excellency,

I write in the spirit of friendship that exists between your country and mine to inquire about the health of ............ She sustained grave injuries when she was arrested in February of this year and is still in hospital.

I am a medical student and as such I am particularly concerned about those needing medical care. But my concern about ............ goes further. She was among hundreds reported arrested during the recent national strike. I take no position on the merits of the strike or the demands of the strikers, nor do I question the policies of your government. I am concerned about human rights.

............ was taken into custody while exercising her rights to freedom of assembly and expression. I urge that she, and all those against whom no criminal charges can be brought, be unconditionally released. As I believe she is in need of urgent medical attention, she should be freed immediately so that she can be treated by doctors of her own choice.

Yours respectfully and sincerely,

## SAMPLE LETTER F

Your Excellency,

I understand that the penal code of your country provides the death penalty for a number of crimes. I regard this punishment as cruel, inhuman and degrading and I believe it should be abolished universally.

The death penalty contradicts the principle of rehabilitation. It can be inflicted on the innocent and has never been shown to have a special deterrent effect. It is contrary to humane values and can have a brutalizing effect on any society that uses it.

I should stress that my concern is based entirely on respect for human life and is not political. I believe we must take every possible step to eradicate violence against human beings, including the taking of life by society itself. It is in this spirit that I urge you to take the lead in ending death sentences and executions in your country.

Yours truly,

## SAMPLE LETTER G

Your Excellency,

I am writing to Your Excellency about the case of ............, who was recently sentenced to death by (name of court, date of sentence).

I understand that this case may be the subject of judicial appeals. However, I am writing to urge, respectfully, that should these appeals be exhausted and the case come before Your Excellency for review, that Your Excellency exercise clemency on humanitarian grounds.

Amnesty International, of which I am a member, opposes the death penalty in all cases on the grounds that it violates the right to life and the right not to be subjected to cruel, inhuman or degrading treatment or punishment as proclaimed in the Universal Declaration of Human Rights.

Yours sincerely and respectfully,

## SAMPLE LETTER H

*(Your group has been working on an investigation case for three years. No reply has been received to any of your letters. You write regularly each month, asking about a different aspect of the case. This time you are going to ask again about the prisoner's place of detention. You write to the Minister of Justice.)*

Dear Minister,

I wish to draw your attention to the fact that I have received no reply from your ministry to a number of letters concerning ............ I write now to ask for information about her place of detention.

............ is reported to have been detained on 3 May 1980 under the Regulations for the Suppression of Rebellion. She was last seen in the custody of officers of the State Security Police. There has been no announcement of any charges against her and no report of any legal proceedings.

Amnesty International, of which I am a member, has taken an interest in this case. It acts in defence of people imprisoned in violation of the Universal Declaration of Human Rights and is seeking details as to the whereabouts of ............

It may interest you to know that, in addition to making inquiries about this case, the Amnesty International group to which I belong is also working for the release of ............, who has been held without trial for seven years in ............, and is campaigning against other human rights abuses in ............

I should be grateful if your ministry would let me know without further delay the whereabouts of ............

Yours respectfully and sincerely,

## SAMPLE TELEGRAMS

A. Respectfully urge immediate medical care for ............ arrested by Revolutionary Guard 17 May. Now reported seriously ill.

B. Deeply concerned arrest of .......... and reports of possible incommunicado detention. Respectfully urge immediate access to lawyers and relatives.

C. ............ abducted by armed agents. Respectfully appeal for urgent investigation to determine prisoner's whereabouts.

D. Respectfully urge clemency for ............ on humanitarian grounds.

E. Urgently require information lawyer .......... detained 5 December and assurances her physical safety.

F. Strongly urge protection ............ against forcible repatriation to ............ where imprisonment and ill-treatment feared likely.

G. Greatly disturbed disappearance of prisoner ............ removed from cell 16 October. Respectfully seek assurances his safety.

# Chapter 11

# Amnesty International Policy

## Statute of Amnesty International

*(Amended and adopted by the 15th International Council, meeting in Rimini, Italy, 9–12 September 1982)*

### OBJECT

1. CONSIDERING that every person has the right freely to hold and to express his or her convictions and the obligation to extend a like freedom to others, the object of AMNESTY INTERNATIONAL shall be to secure throughout the world the observance of the privisions of the Universal Declaration of Human Rights, by:

    (a) irrespective of political considerations working towards the release of and providing assistance to persons who in violation of the aforesaid provisions are imprisoned, detained or otherwise physically restricted by reason of their political, religious or other conscientiously held beliefs or by reason of their ethnic origin, sex, colour or language, provided that they have not used or advocated violence (hereinafter referred to as "Prisoners of Conscience");

    (b) opposing by all appropriate means the detention of any Prisoners of Conscience or any political prisoners without trial within a reasonable time or any trial procedures relating to such prisoners that do not conform to internationally recognized norms;

    (c) opposing by all appropriate means the imposition and infliction of death penalties and torture or other cruel, inhuman or degrading treatment or punishment of prisoners or other detained or restricted persons whether or not they have used or advocated violence.

### METHODS

2. In order to achieve the aforesaid object, AMNESTY INTERNATIONAL shall:

    (a) at all times maintain an overall balance between its activities in relation to countries adhering to the different world political ideologies and groupings;

    (b) promote as appears appropriate the adoption of constitutions, conventions, treaties and other measures which guarantee the rights contained in the provisions referred to in Article 1 hereof;

    (c) support and publicize the activities of and cooperate with international organizations and agencies which work for the implementation of the aforesaid provisions;

    (d) take all necessary steps to establish an effective organization of sections, affiliated groups and individual members;

    (e) secure the adoption by groups of members or supporters of individual Prisoners of Conscience or entrust to such groups other tasks in support of the object set out in Article 1;

    (f) provide financial and other relief to Prisoners of Conscience and their dependants and to persons who have lately been Prisoners of Conscience or who might reasonably be expected to be Prisoners of Conscience or to become Prisoners of Conscience if convicted or if they were to return to their own countries, and to the dependants of such persons;

    (g) work for the improvement of conditions for Prisoners of Conscience and political prisoners;

(h) provide legal aid, where necessary and possible, to Prisoners of Conscience and to persons who might reasonably be expected to be Prisoners of Conscience or to become Prisoners of Conscience if convicted or if they were to return to their own countries, and, where desirable, send observers to attend the trials of such persons;

(i) publicize the cases of Prisoners of Conscience or persons who have otherwise been subjected to disabilities in violation of the aforesaid provisions;

(j) send investigators, where appropriate, to investigate allegations that the rights of individuals under the aforesaid provisions have been violated or threatened;

(k) make representations to international organizations and to governments whenever it appears that an individual is a Prisoner of Conscience or has otherwise been subjected to disabilities in violation of the aforesaid provisions;

(l) promote and support the granting of general amnesties of which the beneficiaries will include Prisoners of Conscience;

(m) adopt any other appropriate methods for the securing of its object.

## ORGANIZATION

3. AMNESTY INTERNATIONAL shall consist of sections, affiliated groups and individual members.

4. The directive authority for the conduct of the affairs of AMNESTY INTERNATIONAL is vested in the International Council.

5. Between meetings of the International Council, the International Executive Committee shall be responsible for the conduct of the affairs of AMNESTY INTERNATIONAL and for the implementation of the decisions of the International Council.

6. The day-to-day affairs of AMNESTY INTERNATIONAL shall be conducted by the International Secretariat headed by a Secretary General under the direction of the International Executive Committee.

7. The office of the International Secretariat shall be in London or such other place as the International Executive Committee

shall decide and which is ratified by at least one half of the sections.

## SECTIONS

8. A section of AMNESTY INTERNATIONAL may be established in any country, state or territory with the consent of the International Executive Committee. In order to be recognized as such, a section shall (a) prior to its recognition have demonstrated its ability to organize and maintain basic AMNESTY INTERNATIONAL activities, (b) consist of not less than two groups and 20 members, (c) submit its statute to the International Executive Committee for approval, (d) pay such annual fee as may be determined by the International Council, (e) be registered as such with the International Secretariat on the decision of the International Executive Committee. Sections shall take no action on matters that do not fall within the stated object of AMNESTY INTERNATIONAL. The International Secretariat shall maintain a register of sections. Sections shall act in accordance with the working rules and guidelines that are adopted from time to time by the International Council.

9. Groups of not less than five members may, on payment of an annual fee determined by the International Council, become affiliated to AMNESTY INTERNATIONAL or a section thereof. Any dispute as to whether a group should be or remain affiliated shall be decided by the International Executive Committee. An affiliated adoption group shall accept for adoption such prisoners as may from time to time be allotted to it by the International Secretariat, and shall adopt no others as long as it remains affiliated to AMNESTY INTERNATIONAL. No group shall be allotted a Prisoner of Conscience detained in its own country. Each section shall maintain and make available to the International Secretariat a register of affiliated AMNESTY INTERNATIONAL groups. Groups in a country without a section shall be registered with the International Secretariat. Groups shall take no action on matters that do not fall within the stated object of AMNESTY INTERNATIONAL.

Groups shall act in accordance with the working rules and guidelines that are adopted from time to time by the International Council.

## INDIVIDUAL MEMBERSHIP

10. Individuals residing in countries where there is no section may, on payment to the International Secretariat of an annual subscription fee determined by the International Executive Committee, become members of AMNESTY INTERNATIONAL with the consent of the International Executive Committee. In countries where a section exists, individuals may become international members of AMNESTY INTERNATIONAL with the consent of the section and of the International Executive Committee. The International Secretariat shall maintain a register of such members.

11. Deleted.

## INTERNATIONAL COUNCIL

12. The International Council shall consist of the members of the International Executive Committee and of representatives of sections and shall meet at intervals of not more than two years on a date fixed by the International Executive Committee. Only representatives of sections shall have the right to vote on the International Council.

13. All sections shall have the right to appoint one representative to the International Council and in addition may appoint representatives as follows:

        10-49 groups : 1 representative
        50-99 groups : 2 representatives
    100-199 groups : 3 representatives
    200-399 groups : 4 representatives
    400 groups or over : 5 representatives

Sections consisting primarily of individual members rather than groups may as an alternative appoint additional representatives as follows:

        500-2,499 : 1 representative
    2,500 and over : 2 representatives

Only sections having paid in full their annual fee as assessed by the International Council for the previous financial year shall vote at the International Council. This requirement may be waived in whole or in part by the International Council.

14. One representative of each group not forming part of a section may attend a meeting of the International Council as an observer and may speak thereat but shall not be entitled to vote.

15. A section unable to participate in an International Council may appoint a proxy or proxies to vote on its behalf and a section represented by a lesser number of persons than its entitlement under Article 13 hereof may authorize its representative or representatives to cast votes up to its maximum entitlement under Article 13 hereof.

16. Notice of the number of representatives proposing to attend an International Council, and of the appointment of proxies, shall be given to the International Secretariat not later than one month before the meeting of the International Council. This requirement may be waived by the International Executive Committee.

17. A quorum shall consist of the representatives or proxies of not less than one quarter of the sections entitled to be represented.

18. The Chairperson of the International Council and an alternate shall be elected by the preceding International Council. The Chairperson or, in his or her absence, the alternate, shall preside at the International Council. In the absence of the Chairperson and the alternate, the Chairperson of the International Executive Committee or such other person as the International Executive Committee may appoint shall open the proceedings of the International Council which shall elect a Chairperson. Thereafter the elected Chairperson, or such other person as the Chairperson may appoint, shall preside at the International Council.

19. Except as otherwise provided in the Statute, the International Council shall make its decisions by a simple majority of the votes cast. In case of an equality of votes the Chairperson of the International Council shall have a casting vote.

20. The International Council shall be convened by the International Secretariat by notice to all sections and affiliated groups

not later than 90 days before the date thereof.

21. The Chairperson of the International Executive Committee shall at the request of the Committee or of not less than one-third of the sections call an extraordinary meeting of the International Council by giving not less than 21 days' notice in writing to all sections.

22. The International Council shall elect a Treasurer, who shall be a member of the International Executive Committee.

23. The International Council may appoint one or more Honorary Presidents of AMNESTY INTERNATIONAL to hold office for a period not exceeding three years.

24. The agenda for the meetings of the International Council shall be prepared by the International Secretariat under the direction of the Chairperson of the International Executive Committee.

## INTERNATIONAL EXECUTIVE COMMITTEE

25. (a) The International Executive Committee shall consist of the Treasurer, one representative of the staff of the International Secretariat and seven regular members, who shall be members of AMNESTY INTERNATIONAL, or of a section, or of an affiliated group. The regular members and Treasurer shall be elected by the International Council by the direct proportional system of election. Not more than one member of any section or affiliated group or AMNESTY INTERNATIONAL member voluntarily resident in a country may be elected as a regular member to the Committee, and once such member has received sufficient votes to be elected, any votes cast for other members of that section, affiliated group or country shall be disregarded.

(b) Members of the permanent staff, paid and unpaid, shall have the right to elect one representative among the staff who has completed not less than two years' service to be a voting member of the International Executive Committee. Such member shall hold office for one year and shall be eligible for re-election. The method of voting shall be subject to approval by the International Executive Committee on the proposal of the staff members.

26. The International Executive Committee shall meet not less than twice a year at a place to be decided by itself.

27. (a) Those members of the International Executive Committee elected by the 15th International Council in 1982 shall be elected for one year only and shall be eligible for re-election.
(b) Members of the International Executive Committee, other than the representative of the staff, shall hold office for a period of two years and shall be eligible for re-election for a maximum tenure of three consecutive terms.

28. The Committee may co-opt not more than two additional members who shall hold office until the close of the next meeting of the International Council; they shall be eligible to be reco-opted once. Co-opted members shall not have the right to vote.

29. In the event of a vacancy occurring on the Committee, other than in respect of the representative of the staff, it may co-opt a further member to fill the vacancy until the next meeting of the International Council, which shall elect such members as are necessary to replace retiring members and to fill the vacancy. In the event of a vacancy occurring on the Committee in respect of the representative of the staff, the staff shall have the right to elect a successor representative to fill the unexpired term of office.

30. If a member of the Committee is unable to attend a meeting, such member may appoint an alternate.

31. The Committee shall each year appoint one of its members to act as Chairperson.

32. The Chairperson may, and at the request of the majority of the Committee shall, summon meetings of the Committee.

33. A quorum shall consist of not less than five members of the Committee or their alternates.

34. The agenda for meetings of the Committee shall be prepared by the International Secretariat under the direction of the Chairperson.

35. The Committee may make regulations for the conduct of the affairs of AMNESTY INTERNATIONAL and for the procedure to be followed at the International Council.

## INTERNATIONAL SECRETARIAT

36. The International Executive Committee may appoint a Secretary General who shall be responsible under its direction for the conduct of the affairs of AMNESTY INTERNATIONAL and for the implementation of the decisions of the International Council.

37. The Secretary General may, after consultation with the Chairperson of the International Executive Committee, and subject to confirmation by that Committee, appoint such executive and professional staff as are necessary for the proper conduct of the affairs of AMNESTY INTERNATIONAL, and may appoint such other staff as are necessary.

38. In the case of the absence or illness of the Secretary General, or of a vacancy in the post of Secretary General, the Chairperson of the International Executive Committee shall, after consultation with the members of that Committee, appoint an Acting Secretary General to act until the next meeting of the Committee.

39. The Secretary General or Acting Secretary General and such members of the International Secretariat as may appear to the Chairperson of the International Executive Committee to be necessary shall attend meetings of the International Council and of the International Executive Committee and may speak thereat but shall not be entitled to vote.

## TERMINATION OF MEMBERSHIP

40. Membership of or affiliation to AMNESTY INTERNATIONAL may be terminated at any time by resignation in writing.

41. The International Council may, upon the proposal of the International Executive Committee or of a section, by a three-fourths majority of the votes cast, deprive a section, an affiliated group or a member of membership of AMNESTY INTERNATIONAL if in its opinion that section, affiliated group or member does not act within the spirit of the object and methods set out in Articles 1 and 2 or does not organize and maintain basic AMNESTY INTERNATIONAL activities or does not observe any of the provisions of this Statute. Before taking such action, all sections shall be informed and the Secretary General shall also inform the section, affiliated group or member of the grounds on which it is proposed to deprive it or such person of membership, and such section, affiliated group or member shall be provided with an opportunity of presenting its or such member's case to the International Council.

42. Deleted.

## FINANCE

43. An auditor appointed by the International Council shall annually audit the accounts of AMNESTY INTERNATIONAL, which shall be prepared by the International Secretariat and presented to the International Executive Committee and the International Council.

44. No part of the income or property of AMNESTY INTERNATIONAL shall directly or indirectly be paid or transferred otherwise than for valuable and sufficient consideration to any of its members by way of dividend, gift, division, bonus or otherwise howsoever by way of profit.

## AMENDMENTS OF STATUTE

45. The Statute may be amended by the International Council by a majority of not less than two-thirds of the votes cast. Amendments may be submitted by the International Executive Committee or by a section. Proposed amendments shall be submitted to the International Secretariat not less than three* months before the International Council meets, and presentation to the International Council shall be supported in writing by at least five sections. Proposed amendments shall be communicated by the International Secretariat to all sections and to members of the International Executive Committee.

*nine months after the 16th International Council in 1983. This amendment was agreed at the 15th International Council, meeting in Rimini, Italy, 9-12 September 1982.

# Impartiality and the Defence of Human Rights

*(This explanation of AI's policy of impartiality is issued by the organization's International Executive Committee. It outlines the ways in which AI endeavours to maintain independence, universality and impartiality in its work.)*

The impartial approach of AI to the defence of specific human rights is based upon the provisions of the Universal Declaration of Human Rights, adopted by the General Assembly of the United Nations on 10 December 1948. The declaration proclaims that the recognition of the inherent dignity and of the equal and inalienable rights of all members of the human family is the foundation of freedom, justice and peace in the world. This faith in the universality of fundamental human rights is one of the principles which the peoples of the United Nations have pledged themselves to uphold and observe in the Charter.

The state, having an international duty to guarantee and enforce human rights, does not "bestow" these rights upon its individual citizens at its own pleasure nor can it retract them at its own will and political convenience. Indeed the very concept of *human rights* implies their inalienable applicability to each human being in all situations (except certain specific cases recognized in international law) without distinction of any kind, such as race, colour, sex, language, religion, political or other opinion, national or social origin, property, birth or other status. Fundamental human rights, therefore, are ends rather than means. In the world of international politics it is a perennial temptation to use human rights as an issue to be exploited, to score points in an international power game. Only when human rights are understood as ends in themselves will the violations of human rights be approached universally, impartially and constructively.

AI is an international movement organized to protect those provisions of the Universal Declaration of Human Rights which fall within its mandate, or in the words of the declaration "to secure their universal and effective recognition and observance".

In fulfilling this mandate, it is therefore of the utmost importance that AI should have no political, religious, racial or other bias. Ever since it was founded in 1961, AI has endeavoured to ensure this by taking practical steps to guarantee the independence, universality and impartiality of its work.

## INDEPENDENCE

AI was founded in 1961 following an appeal launched by British lawyer Peter Benenson in an article entitled "The Forgotten Prisoners" published in the *Observer* magazine on 28 May of that year. Within a month of the publication of his appeal he had received over a thousand offers of support to collect information on cases, to publicize them and approach governments. Within two months, people from five countries had established the beginnings of an international movement.

Today, AI remains the only organization of its kind in the world. It has some 2,500 groups and sections in some 40 countries in Africa, Asia, the Middle East, North America and Latin America, and individual members in more than 100 others.

AI is a non-governmental organization having formal relations with the United Nations (ECOSOC), UNESCO, the Council of Europe, the Organization of American States and the Organization of African Unity. It is not an intergovernmental body and is not subject to governmental control or influence.

The policy of AI is determined by its International Council, the supreme governing body comprising representatives of the movement's sections. This body, which functions on a democratic basis, elects an International Executive Committee which is responsible for the conduct of the affairs of AI and for the implementation of the decisions of the International Council.

AI is financially independent. It is funded by

its members throughout the world and by donations. In order to maintain its independence and impartiality, the International Council of AI has established strict guidelines for the acceptance of funds to guarantee that "any funds received by AI (its secretariat, sections, committees and groups) must in no way compromise the integrity of the principles for which AI works, limit the freedom of activity and expression enjoyed by the organization or restrict its areas of concern." The AI accounts are audited annually and are published in the annual report of the organization.

## UNIVERSALITY

The working methods of AI reflect the fundamental belief that responsibility for the protection of human rights transcends differences of nationality, race or belief. Unlike domestic civil liberties organizations, AI groups work on an international basis. This parallels the evolution of international human rights legislation in the past two decades which has established the principle that the defence of human rights is of concern to the entire international community.

AI is committed to taking action wherever and whenever information about violations of human rights falling within its mandate comes to its attention. The availability of such information is therefore an important factor in determining the universality of AI's work. The Research Department of AI compiles and cross-checks information about human rights violations in any country in the world from a wide variety of sources. It uses the international press, transcriptions of radio announcements, official governmental statements and interviews with government officials, reports from legal experts, letters from prisoners' relatives, friends and colleagues, affidavits, and unsolicited contacts in numerous countries. It also relies on the information provided by its fact-finding missions to assess situations on the spot, to meet prisoners and to interview government authorities.

Several factors affect the availability of information and consequently the breadth of AI's reports. For example, there are reasons to believe that in a number of countries gross violations of human rights occur on a large scale as a consequence of administrative policy. But often in these cases the corroborative information necessary for AI reports cannot be obtained. AI thus runs the risk of being misunderstood as giving an unbalanced view of the situation in the world as a whole but cannot for that reason go beyond its practice of drawing attention to specific human rights violations whenever it obtains substantial information.

## IMPARTIALITY

The work of AI is based on the support of a mass membership and involves interventions with governments of all political persuasions, and collaboration with and action through both intergovernmental and non-governmental organizations. It is therefore essential that AI should command the confidence and respect of all these categories and should not only be, but be seen by them to be, impartial.

Article 2(a) of the organization's Statute requires AI to "at all times maintain an overall balance between its activities in relation to countries adhering to the different world political ideologies and groupings".

When examining the overall impartiality of the movement, it is important to bear in mind that AI has at its disposal a considerable variety of techniques to respond to human rights violations. These have evolved on the basis of practical experience of working for prisoners. The techniques include letters to government authorities, appeals which may take the form of general petitions addressed to a head of state and signed by thousands of individuals, appeals from professional associations or prominent personalities, public declarations or statements by international institutions, delegations to embassies, meetings with visiting foreign officials, representations by sections to their own governments seeking increased international diplomatic pressure in defence of human rights. Both through its International Secretariat and its sections, AI issues statements to the news media, maintains a publications program and organizes campaigns on specific themes and countries. This is in addition to the traditional core of the organization's program: the adoption of individual prisoners of conscience.

In its case work (the movement handles more than 4,000 individual cases of prisoners of conscience each year), AI's impartiality is emphasized by the requirement that local groups should at any one time adopt at least two prisoners of conscience from different regions of the world. When allocating cases, attention is paid to ensuring that sufficient overall political contrast is maintained in the work of each group to demonstrate AI's basic object of working for the release of prisoners of conscience irrespective of political considerations. This is important to preclude any suspicion that the individual AI group (or the whole movement) is politically biased. As a further safeguard, and as a method of internationalizing concern for human rights, groups are never assigned individual cases of prisoners of conscience in their own country.

This principle is extended to the Campaign for Prisoners of the Month and to Prisoners of Conscience Week in which the cases are very carefully selected to reflect the political impartiality of AI's work. In the Campaign for Prisoners of the Month, for example, AI selects three cases of prisoners of conscience who are in special need of outside help. These prisoners may be ill or have been detained under severe conditions for a prolonged period of time. The details of these critical cases are included in the monthly *Amnesty International Newsletter* and sent to AI members for immediate action. The practice of working for prisoners of conscience from contrasting political systems is carefully maintained. This policy has proved effective on purely pragmatic grounds. At no time does AI presume either to rank or to compare violations of human rights, nor does AI intend any judgment that violations of human rights are similar or comparable under any political system.

The Borderline Committee also illustrates the principle of impartiality that permeates the working of AI. It is a permanent body responsible for reviewing any case referred to it by the International Secretariat for advice as to whether the case fulfils the statutory requirements for adoption or investigation as a prisoner of conscience. Its members are appointed by the International Executive Committee from three different sections or countries.

Often AI responds unostentatiously. For example, if it appears that public intervention may harm the prisoner or the family, private approaches may have to be made to the authorities concerned. At other times, it may be more effective for AI to work for prisoners of conscience by pressing governments through other organizations or institutions, through commercial, professional or religious organizations which are concerned with protecting the interests of their members; for example, doctors, lawyers, agricultural workers, steel workers, school teachers or journalists.

On the other hand, there are human rights violations which call for a massive public outcry. In these situations AI seeks to awaken world public opinion boldly and openly. Each technique is applied on a country-by-country basis in order to achieve maximum effectiveness. For instance, when appropriate, AI organizes extensive public action on behalf of prisoners in countries where there are a large number of well-documented violations of human rights, even if it is not in a position to launch similar action elsewhere for lack of substantiated information. This bears out the fact that AI will act only on accurate information and, as stipulated in the Statute, "irrespective of political consideration".

# Amnesty International and the Use of Violence

## AN EXPLANATORY NOTE

*This explanation of AI's policy on the use of violence for political ends is based on a statement prepared by a sub-committee established by its International Council in Vienna in 1973. The sub-committee was asked to consider the question of violence within AI's Statute.*

AI was founded essentially to work for the release of those who were detained in violation of the Universal Declaration of Human Rights and who had *not used or advocated violence*. The non-violence clause was thus of the essence of the movement from its foundation, and was an important factor in attracting widespread support from people in all walks of life and of every political persuasion.

Since then, people have frequently queried this restriction and urged that AI's work be extended to those who, according to the pre-amble to the Universal Declaration of Human Rights, have been compelled "to have recourse, as a last resort, to rebellion against tyranny and oppression". The vast majority of the AI member-ship, however, has always remained firmly opposed to the extension of AI's work *for the release of prisoners* to those who have been involved in violence and this position is in fact generally understood and accepted by those outside the movement.

The explanations and justifications for this position can be summed up as follows:

## AI MAY ACT FOR THOSE WHO HAVE BEEN INVOLVED IN VIOLENCE

The reproach that AI refuses to concern itself with prisoners who have been compelled to have resort to violence is based on a misunder-standing. AI's work now has three aspects:

1.  The release of prisoners of conscience (that is, non-violent prisoners).
2.  A fair trial within a reasonable time for *all political prisoners*.
3.  The humane treatment of *all prisoners*.

These last two aspects of its work have assumed growing importance as the movement has expan-ded. Thus, AI intervenes through a variety of techniques to prevent the imposition of the death penalty on, or the torture or ill-treatment of, all prisoners, whether involved in violence or not.

Furthermore, AI will not necessarily consider a prisoner excluded from its definition of prisoner of conscience unless he or she has been convicted of offences involving the use or advocacy of violence after a fair trial in a court of law. In the case of prisoners, whether accused or suspected of violence or not, who have been detained for a long period without trial, it may intervene to seek to ensure their trial or release. Also, a prisoner may be adopted if he or she is kept in detention after completing his or her sentence for an act of violence. All that the

"violence clause" means in practice is that AI will not ask a government to release a prisoner while he or she is serving a sentence imposed after a fair trial for activities involving violence. For the reasons set out below, this restriction seems essential for the effectiveness of the organization.

## AI TAKES NO MORAL STAND ON THE ISSUE OF VIOLENCE

It sometimes seems to be thought that AI, as an organization, is opposed to the use of violence in any circumstances. This is not so. AI's position is entirely impartial. AI was not founded to work for general economic, social and political justice in the various countries of the world — however much its individual members may wish to do so, and are free to do so through other bodies —but to bring relief to individual victims of injustice. It has been built up to do this, and is uniquely equipped to do it. The question of whether resort to violence is justified or not is extraneous to this central task.

It is, however, clear that the extension of AI's work to action for the release of prisoners convicted of violence would compromise the effectiveness of its work both for prisoners of conscience and for prisoners involved in vio-lence. This, and not a moral stand, is the reason for the "violence clause".

## A QUESTION OF EFFECTIVENESS

AI's work is based on the support of a mass membership and involves interventions with governments of all political persuasions, and collaboration with and action through inter-national organizations, both governmental and non-governmental. It is therefore essential that AI should command the confidence and respect of all these categories and should not only be, but be seen by them to be, impartial.

AI now has more than 350,000 active members and supporters of all political affili-ations, pacifists as well as people convinced that in some or many parts of the world violence is the only means of overcoming the even greater violence now being practised by those in power. From this point of view the clause is basically a necessary limitation to enable people of all political colours to work together.

Although most members would probably consider as individuals that there are some situations where violent action is the only solution, the membership would not agree on what those situations are. AI's membership must be universal, and include members of the right willing to intervene in countries with a government of the right and members of the left willing to intervene in countries with a government of the left. Interventions of this kind are clearly more effective than those by the prisoner's political sympathizers.

With regard to governments, AI's influence depends on the fact that governments accept it as an independent organization, politically impartial in relation both to it and to its opposition. If AI began to demand the release of those who have been involved in violent opposition to the government it would become identified with the opposition in the government's mind and lose its credit and its influence. Not only would such demands for release be ineffective, but its work for non-violent prisoners and for the humane treatment of those who have used violence would suffer.

Similarly, AI's standing with international organizations — such as the United Nations, ECOSOC, UNESCO, the Organization of African Unity, the Organization of American States and the Council of Europe — would be endangered, and its initiatives (for example, in relation to the status of conscientious objectors in the Council of Europe and in relation to torture at the United Nations) would lose the authority which comes from its independence and impartiality.

Finally, if AI became identified in governments' minds with certain opposition groups, its value to those very opposition groups would be diminished. At the present time, they are able to and do refer to AI pronouncements as those of an outside, impartial body to whose views the government will attach more weight than to their own. Further, members of such groups have, when AI's position is explained to them, fully accepted it, and recognize that it is a condition of AI's effectiveness in the fields in which it does seek to help them.

## A PRACTICAL PROBLEM

While it is a secondary consideration, it is certain that the problems of delineating violent political actions as against violent criminal actions would be almost insuperable and subject to all manner of subjective political preconceptions. Would all kinds of violent actions be covered? Hijackings, kidnappings, the killing of hostages, bombing causing the deaths of innocent people? Who would draw the distinctions? And who would decide, and on what criteria, that resort to violence was justifiable? The introduction of such concepts would inevitably lead to dissensions on the basis of the political beliefs of the membership which, under the present system, can remain irrelevant to the individual's action as a member of AI.

## AN ARGUMENT OF PRINCIPLE

It must be remembered that one aspect of AI's work is to ensure humane (that is, non-violent) treatment for political prisoners. AI would be applying a double standard if it insisted that the police and prison authorities abstain from any act of violence or brutality yet maintained that those on the other side should be allowed to commit such acts and yet be unpunished. It can and does insist that punishment should be humanely carried out, but it would discredit itself if it maintained that the very violence which it is seeking to eliminate from police practices is justified when used by the opposition.

# Policy Guidelines on Conscientious Objection

*(Revised and adopted by the 13th International Council, Vienna, 1980)*

1. A conscientious objector is understood to be a person liable to conscription for military service who, for reasons of conscience or profound conviction arising from religious, ethical, moral, humanitarian, philosophical, political or similar motives refuses to perform

armed service or any other direct or indirect participation in wars or armed conflicts.

2. Where a person is detained/imprisoned because he or she claims that he or she on the grounds of conscience described in paragraph 1 above objects to military service, Amnesty International will consider him or her a Prisoner of Conscience, if his or her imprisonment/detention is a consequence of one or more of the following reasons:

(a) the legal code of a country does not contain provisions for the recognition of conscientious objection and for a person to register his or her objection at a specific point in time;

(b) a person is refused the right to register his or her objection;

(c) the recognition of conscientious objection is so restricted that only some and not all of the above-mentioned grounds of conscience or profound conviction are acceptable;

(d) a person does not have the right to claim conscientious objection on the above-mentioned grounds of conscience or profound conviction developed after conscription into the armed forces;

(e) he or she is imprisoned as a consequence of his or her leaving the armed forces without authorization for reasons of conscience developed after conscription into the armed forces, if he or she has taken such reasonable steps to secure his or her release by lawful means as might grant him or her release from the military obligations on the grounds of conscience or if he or she did not use those means because he or she has been deprived of reasonable access to the knowledge of them;

(f) there is not a right to alternative service outside the "war machine";

(g) the length of the alternative service is deemable as a punishment for his or her conscientious objection.

3. A person should not be considered a Prisoner of Conscience if he or she is not willing to state the reason for his or her refusal to perform military service, unless it can be inferred from all the circumstances of the case that the refusal is based on conscientious objection.

4. A person should however not be considered a Prisoner of Conscience if he or she is offered and refuses comparable alternative service outside the "war machine".

# Declaration of Stockholm

*(Adopted by the Amnesty International Conference on the Abolition of the Death Penalty, Stockholm, December 1977)*

The Stockholm Conference on the Abolition of the Death Penalty, composed of more than 200 delegates and participants from Africa, Asia, Europe, the Middle East, North and South America and the Caribbean region,

**RECALLS THAT:**
— The death penalty is the ultimate cruel, inhuman and degrading punishment and violates the right to life.

**CONSIDERS THAT:**
— The death penalty is frequently used as an instrument of repression against opposition, racial, ethnic, religious and underprivileged groups,
— Execution is an act of violence, and violence tends to provoke violence,

— The imposition and infliction of the death penalty is brutalizing to all who are involved in the process,
— The death penalty has never been shown to have a special deterrent effect,
— The death penalty is increasingly taking the form of unexplained "disappearances", extra-judicial executions and political murders,
— Execution is irrevocable and can be inflicted on the innocent.

**AFFIRMS THAT:**
— It is the duty of the state to protect the life of all persons within its jurisdiction without exception,

— Executions for the purposes of political coercion, whether by government agencies or

others, are equally unacceptable,
— Abolition of the death penalty is imperative for the achievement of declared international standards.

**DECLARES:**
— Its total and unconditional opposition to the death penalty,
— Its condemnation of all executions, in whatever form, committed or condoned by governments,
— Its commitment to work for the universal abolition of the death penalty.

**CALLS UPON:**
— Non-governmental organizations, both national and international, to work collectively and individually to provide public information materials directed towards the abolition of the death penalty,

— All governments to bring about the immediate and total abolition of the death penalty,

— The United Nations unambiguously to declare that the death penalty is contrary to international law.

# Guidelines for Sections and Groups

*These guidelines for the work of AI sections and groups were adopted by the 15th International Council, 1982. For explanatory notes to these guidelines, see Report of the 15th International Council, AI Index: ORG 52/01/82.*

### Minimum Requirements for Sections

**1.** A section must have a statute which reflects the objects and methods of AI as contained in the AI Statute. This statute is to be approved by the International Executive Committee.

**2.** A section must have an active membership, not less than two groups and 20 members, which in promotion of AI's mandated concerns shall maintain a reasonable level of participation in basic AI activities: for example, adoption work, Urgent Actions, the Campaign for the Prisoners of the Month, country campaigns.

**3.** A section must act in accordance with the AI Statute and the Working Rules and guidelines adopted from time to time by the International Council and the International Executive Committee. Of particular importance are the guidelines regarding security and responsible handling of information and the guidelines on section work on one's own country. A section shall take no action on matters that do not fall within these provisions.

**4.** A section must not operate in violation of the law of its own country.

**5.** A section's composition and the circumstances in which it operates must be such as to ensure its political independence and freedom of action.

**6.** A section must have a reasonable number of members who have undergone a basic training in the aims and methods of Amnesty International. This training will normally be by participation in internationally accepted training programs; it may also take place, where appropriate, through visits to the International Secretariat, through work in other sections, or through visits by IS staff or experienced AI members.

**7.** A section should be able to deal with material in the working language of the international movement (English).

**8.** A section must have a governing body, such as an executive committee or board, which represents the membership of the section and which meets regularly.

**9.** A section must submit comprehensive annual reports on its activities to the International Executive Committee.

**10.** A section shall make such financial contribution to the international movement as is determined by the International Council.

**11.**   A section must ensure its financial independence and observe AI international guidelines on acceptance of financial contributions and fund-raising.

**12.**   A section must submit annual statements of its finances to the Treasurer.

## Notes

(a)   Recognition: a section is recognized in accordance with Article 8 of the AI Statute. In order to fulfil and demonstrate continuous adherence to the minimum requirements for a section, a potential section should participate in AI work for not less than one year before seeking recognition by the International Executive Committee.

(b)   Temporary or permanent closure: external changes in the political circumstances in which a section exists and operates or internal developments within the section which seriously affect one or more of the minimum requirements may lead to the temporary closure of the section by the International Executive Committee or its permanent closure by the International Council.

(c)   Exemption: any one or all of the guidelines for sections and groups may be waived by the International Executive Committee in relation to a particular section or group, where considered advisable or necessary in the existing circumstances.

## Responsibilities of a Section

**1.**   The section through its governing body is responsible to the International Executive Committee for the proper functioning of the AI organization in that country and for ensuring consistent and effective work for concerns within the AI mandate.

**2.**   The section is responsible for participating in the consultation and decision-making process of the international organization and for implementing relevant International Council decisions.

**3.**   The section is responsible for promoting awareness of the work and aims of Amnesty International on a national level.

**4.**   The section is responsible for ensuring that the impartiality and political balance of Amnesty International is reflected in the work and image of the section in the country.

**5.**   The section is responsible for recruiting new members and for preparing programs for developing membership from a broad spectrum of the community.

**6.**   The section is responsible for ensuring that its members are informed of and act in accordance with the mandate of the organization and with its Working Rules and internal guidelines including those related to security, responsible handling of information and work on one's own country.

**7.**   The section is responsible for developing membership training programs and materials.

**8.**   The section is responsible for establishing, closing and monitoring the activities of adoption groups, coordination groups, professional groups and any other membership structure it may develop within its own country.

**9.**   The section is responsible for maintaining up-to-date membership records and mailing lists and should make these available to the International Secretariat if requested.

**10.**   The section is responsible for informing the International Secretariat of the names of the officers and staff of the section and for notifying the International Secretariat of any change of address of the section or groups within the section.

**11.**   The section is responsible for the handling of material sent to it by the International Secretariat and for making AI information available to the members and to the general public as appropriate.

**12.**   The section is responsible for the distribution of the AI Newsletter and other AI publications in its own country and for developing subscriber programs as appropriate.

**13.**   The section is responsible where appropriate for developing a program of translation into national languages.

**14.**   The section is responsible for developing fund-raising activities in its own country.

**15.**   The section is responsible for developing relations with the national press and with national organizations and institutions. It is also responsible for preparing guidelines for use by its members in these relations.

**16.**   The section is normally responsible for

contacts with its own government, apart from approaches about human rights violations within the government's jurisdiction which are the responsibilities of the International Executive Committee and the International Secretariat.

*Minimum Requirements for AI Groups* (within sections and in countries or territories where there is no section)

**1.** The group shall be registered with the section, or where there is no section, with the International Secretariat.

**2.** The group must have an organized structure and sufficient active members—not less than five—to ensure effective and continuous work, to elect officers, and to maintain a reliable mailing address. In particular where there is no section, some of its members need to be able to deal with material in the working language of the international movement (English).

**3.** All members of the group shall agree to work in accordance with the AI Statute and the Working Rules and guidelines adopted from time to time by the International Council, the International Executive Committee and the section, as appropriate. Of particular importance are the guidelines regarding security and responsible handling of information and the guidelines on section work in one's own country.

**4.** From an early stage of the formation of the group its members shall participate in AI training programs in order to gain a clear understanding of AI's aims and working methods and to develop training programs for new members.

**5.** The group shall maintain a reasonable and consistent level of AI activity in promotion of AI's mandated concerns and shall submit reports on its work every six months to the section and, where necessary, to the International Secretariat. Where there is no section, a group shall submit its reports to the International Secretariat.

**6.** The group must acquire a sound financial basis so as to ensure its financial participation in the movement. It must safeguard its financial independence through observance of AI international guidelines on acceptance of financial contributions and fund-raising.

**7.** The group must not operate in violation of the law of its own country.

**8.** The composition of the group and the circumstances in which it operates must be such as to ensure its political independence and freedom of action. This is of particular importance for a group where there is no section.

*Notes*

(a) *Recognition.* A group shall be formed and recognized only with the consent of the section, or where there is no section, with the consent of the International Executive Committee.

(b) *Temporary or permanent closure.* Temporary or permanent closure of a group where there is a section is governed by the rules for groups of the respective section. Where there is no section, external changes in the political circumstances in which the group exists and operates or internal developments within the group which seriously affect one or more of the above minimum requirements may lead to the temporary or permanent closure of the group by the International Executive Committee.

*Public Role of Members of Section Governing Bodies and Senior Staff Members*

In order to maintain the independence of sections, it is recommended to adopt the following rules:

**1.** To be a member of a section governing body or a senior staff member is incompatible with holding an elected or appointed top level position in the administrative, policy-making, law-giving, defence and law enforcement system of a country; it is also incompatible with holding other elected or appointed positions which play a determinant role in foreign policy or domestic law enforcement decisions of a country.

**2.** To be a member of a section governing body or a senior staff member is incompatible with holding a position in top ruling bodies of political parties.

**3.** An AI member should not accept membership of a section governing body or a senior staff position while holding any of the above-mentioned positions. If elected or accepting appointment to any such post he or she should resign from the section governing body or senior staff position.

**4.** In some situations a person's previous employment or activity may prove incompatible with being a member of a section governing body or senior staff member.

**5.** In any situation of uncertainty as to whether or not a present position or previously held position should be treated as coming within the above rules, the section and/or the member concerned should seek and abide by the opinion of the International Executive Committee.

**6.** These guidelines also apply to leading members of AI groups in countries or territories without a section.

*Notes*

(a) Somewhat similar guidelines were adopted in September 1979 by the International Executive Committee regarding the public roles of International Executive Committee members.

(b) Sections may want to draw up for themselves similar guidelines which would relate to appointment or election of individuals to posts within the section at local and regional levels.

(c) The International Executive Committee will take these guidelines into consideration when approving the creation of groups without a section.

# Guidelines on AI Sections' Activities concerning Human Rights Violations in their Own Countries

*(Adopted by the 12th International Council, Leuven, 1979)*

Amnesty International was founded in the belief that the protection of human rights is an international and not merely a national responsibility. The working methods of the movement embody this principle and assure that impartiality and independence remain fundamental to all AI activities in defence of the human rights falling within its mandate.

The structure of the AI movement and the division of responsibilities within it are designed to ensure the international consistency and cohesiveness of the movement. All AI sections act as a part of the international movement on the basis of materials provided or approved by the international bodies of the movement.

AI sections in principle have no special obligations in relation to violations of human rights in their own countries. Such violations and actions against them are the concern and the responsibility of the entire movement.

The following guidelines determine the relation of sections and groups to human rights issues falling within the mandate of AI arising in the country or territory in which the section or group is situated.

These guidelines are designed to ensure that local interests and pressures in no way influence or appear to influence the impartiality of AI's judgment, to demonstrate unambiguously the principle of international responsibility underlying the movement and to maintain the distinction between AI's purpose and working methods and those of domestic civil liberties bodies.

## 1. INDIVIDUAL CASES

(a) No group or section shall be involved in work for or appeals on behalf of an individual prisoner or group of prisoners imprisoned or detained in the country or territory of that group or section.

(b) This principle shall apply to cases of known or possible prisoners of conscience as well as to known or possible victims of torture, cruel, inhuman or degrading treatment or punishment, including the death penalty, and to cases of political prisoners detained without trial or subjected to procedures that do not conform to internationally recognized norms.

(c) Any exception to this procedure shall be decided by the International Executive

Committee (IEC) in consultation with the section concerned. Any such exception shall be permitted by the IEC only in the best interests of the prisoners.

(d) A section may request, for its own information, a list of prisoners imprisoned or detained in the section's own country or territory, whose cases have been taken up by AI for adoption or investigation. This information will be provided by the International Secretariat, subject to considerations of security and confidentiality.

(e) A section shall be notified automatically upon request of any action to be taken by the international movement on behalf of an individual case involving the death penalty in the section's own country or territory.

## 2. REPRESENTATIONS TO GOVERNMENTS

(a) It is not the responsibility of a section to make representations to its government concerning human rights violations in its own country. Such representations are the responsibility of the IEC and of other sections acting on the basis of information provided by the IS.

(b) A section may only make representations to its own government concerning violations of human rights in its own country or territory if authorized to do so by the IEC. In making any such representation, after authorization by the IEC, the section should always make it clear that its own action in this regard reflects the concern of the international movement as a whole.

(c) A section may make representations to the appropriate authorities in its own country or territory relating to ratification of treaties and changes in legislation, relating to the death penalty and relating to refugees, in accordance with guidelines 3, 4 and 8 respectively.

## 3. RATIFICATION OF TREATIES AND CHANGES IN LEGISLATION

(a) A section may make representations to its own government with a view to persuading the government to sign, ratify or accede to international treaties in the field of human rights or to change or refrain from changing legislation relating to the death penalty. These activities, including public statements relating to such activities, do not require authorization from the IEC. A section may seek changes in the legislation in its own country or territory with a view to bringing the legislation into conformity with standards laid down by international law, and may oppose proposed changes derogating from such standards. It may also seek changes in its national legislation concerning other specific matters falling within the statutory concerns of AI. These representations and any public statements relating to such representations shall be made with the advance agreement of the IEC. Such advance agreement of the IEC may be given in relation to specific representations or public statements related to such representations or generally.

## 4. DEATH PENALTY

(a) A section may work towards the abolition of the death penalty and against legislation to reintroduce it in its own country. A section may make representations to its own government concerning changes in legislation and ratification of international covenants and treaties relating to the death penalty. These activities do not require authorization from the IEC.

(b) In making representations to its own government with regard to the death penalty, a section may illustrate its point with individual cases from its own country in conjunction with cases from other countries.

(c) No action may be taken by a section on behalf of an individual case of the death penalty in its own country or territory. Any exception to this procedure shall be decided by the IEC in consultation with the section concerned.

(d) No section is required to collect information on the death penalty in its own country. However, in the course of its activities on the death penalty in its own country, a section may, if it wishes, collect information on the death penalty which it considers useful for the work of the section and of the international movement.

## 5. MISSIONS

(a) It is not the responsibility of a section to request, plan, brief or collaborate with an AI mission sent by the IEC to the country or territory of that section.

(b) A section shall be notified in advance of

the visit of an AI mission to its own country, subject to considerations of security and confidentiality. If a section has been notified of the visit of an AI mission to its country, it may respond to inquiries by confirming the arrival of the mission and stating the general concerns of the mission. The section may make no public statements concerning the mission without the advance agreement of the IEC.

## 6. PUBLIC STATEMENTS AND PUBLICATIONS

(a) Responsibility for the approval of all public statements or publications concerning human rights violations in a country with an AI section rests with the IEC who act on behalf of the international movement. Sections are not empowered to make public statements or to issue publications concerning the human rights situation in their own country. The term "publications" includes news releases, newsletters, articles, films, sound or video tapes and posters.

(b) Any exceptions to this principle shall be decided by the IEC in consultation with the section concerned.

(c) A section may make public statements concerning the ratification of treaties and changes in legislation on the death penalty in accordance with guideline 3.

(d) In response to inquiries about human rights violations in their own country a section shall explain that the responsibility for such action and policy lies with the IEC. The section may refer without further elaboration to any available AI external information. The section may also state that AI has taken action on behalf of individual prisoners, by adoption or investigation, if this is the case and if the section has been notified of the fact.

(e) A section, at its own request, may be provided with copies of AI publications and external documents concerning its own country and may take part in the distribution of such documents.

## 7. COLLECTION OF INFORMATION

(a) It is not the responsibility of any section to investigate or collect information about actual or possible violations of human rights in any country or territory including its own. Such investigations and the evaluation of all information received from any source relating to alleged violations of human rights in any country or territory are the responsibility of the Research Department of the International Secretariat acting under the authority of the International Executive Committee. The IEC can entrust to a section the collection of information on the section's own country, subject to agreement with the section concerned on the nature and scope of the collection of information. The IEC may permit such activity subject to such limitations and safeguards as the IEC considers necessary.

(b) Members of any section may in their personal capacity and not as members of AI forward allegations of human rights violations falling within the mandate of AI in any country, including their own, to the IS. The details of AI's mandate and the address of the IS should always be provided by the section to any individual (whether a member of AI or not) who wishes to communicate such allegations. It is not the function of a section to act as a channel.

(c) In the course of its activities on the death penalty in its own country, a section may, if it wishes, collect information on the death penalty which it considers useful for the work of the section and of the international movement.

(d) No section should make inquiries of a section in another country concerning prisoners or human rights violations in such other country.

## 8. REFUGEES AND ASYLUM

(a) A section may make representations to the appropriate authorities in its own country or territory on individual cases of refugees falling within AI's mandate (people who can reasonably be expected to become prisoners of conscience or to be subjected to torture or politically motivated extrajudicial killing and people who would face the imposition or execution of the judicial death penalty). A section may monitor and make representations on government policy on individual cases or general refugee matters. Sections should consult the IS on any refugee question which is not clearly within AI's mandate and on any cases of assisting people to emigrate.

(b) Any public statement relating to representations to the authorities concerning individual cases shall be made in consultation with the IS. Sections are obliged to inform the IS of any public representations to their government in relation to general refugee matters.

(Adopted by the International Council, 1980)

## 9. RELIEF
(a) It is not the responsibility of any AI section to distribute relief to prisoners and their families in their own country or territory. The AI relief program is maintained by sections and groups providing assistance to individual prisoners allocated to them and by an international relief fund administered by the IS under the authority of the IEC.

(b) Any exception to these procedures shall be determined by the IEC in consultation with the sections concerned.

## 10. PRISON CONDITIONS
(a) Where the prison conditions of an individual prisoner or a group of prisoners is a matter of concern to AI, action shall be taken in accordance with the procedure outlined under "individual cases".

(b) Where questions of national and international legislation are directly relevant to the regulation of prison conditions within a country or territory in which an AI section is situated, the section may make representations to the appropriate bodies with a view to ensuring that domestic legislation conforms to the relevant international standards. These representations and any public statements relating to such representations shall be made with the advance agreement of the IEC. Such advance agreement of the IEC may be given in relation to specific representations or public statements related to such representations or generally.

## APPLICATION OF THE GUIDELINES
These guidelines apply to AI sections and to groups and members in countries without AI sections.

All communication with the IS and the IEC in relation to these guidelines should come from the governing body of the section.

Where authorization is given by the IEC to the governing body of a section, it is recognized that this authorization may include groups and members acting under the authority of the section.

All communication with the IS and the IEC in relation to these guidelines should be channelled through the office of the Secretary General. The IEC may delegate its authority for decision-making to the Secretary General who will at such times be acting on behalf of the IEC. The IEC is responsible for ensuring that communications from sections in connection with these guidelines are dealt with as rapidly as the extent of the required investigations permits.

**Note:** Nothing in these guidelines shall preclude any member of AI from involvement in any issue relating to his or her own country in a private capacity or as a member of any other organization, for example, a domestic civil liberties body, provided that it is made clear that such member is not acting as a member of AI.

# Guidelines for the Acceptance of Financial Contributions and Fund-raising by AI

*(Revised and adopted by the 13th International Council, Vienna, 1980)*

## 1. STATEMENT OF PURPOSE
This document offers guidelines for the raising and receiving of funds by Amnesty International. Their purpose is to safeguard the integrity and independence of the organization by setting forth general principles and regulatory safeguards to guide the relevant decisions of members and the responsible organs of Amnesty International.

## 2. GENERAL PRINCIPLES
(i) AMNESTY INTERNATIONAL IS A HUMANITARIAN ORGANIZATION DEDICATED TO THE DEFENCE OF SPECIFIC HUMAN RIGHTS AS DEFINED BY ITS STATUTE. Hence, funds sought by and given to Amnesty International must be in consonance with the objectives of the Statute.

(ii) AMNESTY INTERNATIONAL IS AND MUST REMAIN A BROADLY BASED AND SELF-SUPPORTING ORGANIZATION. Hence, funds raised and received by Amnesty International must neither narrow nor diminish its volunteer and popular support.

(iii) AMNESTY INTERNATIONAL IS AND MUST REMAIN, AND BE SEEN TO REMAIN, AN INDEPENDENT AND IMPARTIAL ORGANIZATION. Hence, funds requested and accepted by Amnesty International must in no way incur financial dependence, real or apparent, upon any political or interest group singly or in combination, nor limit the freedom of activity and expression enjoyed by the organization, nor direct its areas of concern.

## 3. REGULATORY SAFEGUARDS

(i) No donation with conditions attached that are inconsonant with the Statute is to be accepted by any constituent body of Amnesty International (group, section, International Secretariat, etc).

(ii) Should a constituent body of Amnesty International be offered or receive a donation (or donations) from any single source during a budgetary year which amounts to 5% or more of that body's expected income for that year (and is not less than £100), before final acceptance notification of the gift identifying its source, amount and purpose is to be made as follows:

    (a) For a group or other constituent body of an Amnesty International section, notification is to the governing body of the section, which is to judge the acceptability of the gift in the light of the above general principles (2 i, ii, iii).

    (b) for a section or constituent body of Amnesty International which is not part of a section, notification is to the International Executive Committee, which is to judge the acceptability of the gift in the light of the above general principles (2 i, ii, iii).

NB: Should a constituent body of Amnesty International be offered or receive a donation which amounts to less than 5% of that body's expected income for the budgetary year but whose source, intent or consequence is questionable, notification should be given as prescribed above (3 ii).

(iii) No governmental donations are to be accepted by any constituent body of Amnesty International. An exception to this rule may be made for relief (as noted below (4 iii)).

NB: This regulation always applies to grants from national governments. It also applies to intergovernmental bodies of a regional, subregional or other non-universal nature. Whether other public bodies such as legislatures, local authorities, other intergovernmental organizations or the judiciary are included in the restriction is to be decided by the bodies referred to above (3 ii) when resolving concrete cases which come before them. These bodies are also to decide on the acceptability of benefits other than direct grants from governmental sources, such as tax-exempt status or programs which permit conscientious objectors to work for Amnesty International in lieu of military service.

(iv) Annual financial reports are to be prepared by the constituent bodies of Amnesty International to serve as a public record of income and expenditures. These are to be available on request for public inspection at any time at the international, national and local level.

## 4. OTHER PRECAUTIONS

(i) Funds are not to be accepted from individuals, institutions, or special interest groups for projects in which they have a special stake or when such a contribution can be construed as influencing the means or the ends of the project. Any proposed exception to this rule is subject to the notification rule prescribed above (3 ii).

(ii) Funds are to be neither sought nor accepted from any individual, agency or institution for the purpose of establishing or maintaining a constituent body of Amnesty International (group, section, etc). Any proposed exception to this rule is subject to the notification rule prescribed above (3 ii).

(iii) Funds for relief work, as is customary with humanitarian and charitable organizations, may be sought and received by Amnesty International from the broadest possible spectrum, including governments and governmental agencies. The use of such relief funds is to be administered directly by Amnesty International and should be sought or received only on this basis. Such funds will be distributed according to the Policies and Procedures adopted by the International Council.

(iv) Anonymous donations where so desired can be made to Amnesty International in accordance with generally accepted practices of charitable organizations. Within the juris-diction of a section they are to be received at the discretion of the governing body of the section, and in all other cases at the discretion of the International Executive Committee. In each instance judgment must be made in accordance with the principles (2 i, ii, iii) and regulations (3 i, ii, iii, iv) set forth in these guidelines.

## Keep your group going . . .

Your local AI group is the focus for AI's campaign in your community. Public understanding and support is vital. You need to keep up the publicity, letter writing and appeals on behalf of the cases allocated to your group. You need to build public support for the campaigns in which your group participates. You need to recruit new members and raise money.

Don't overlook the schools, community centres and local authorities in your area. Don't forget the trade unions, religious bodies, sports clubs or shopping centres. Each gives an opportunity for your group to carry AI's message to a wider public. If our campaign is to succeed, we need many more people with us: writing letters, signing petitions, handing out leaflets and contributing the funds and energy that will give even greater impact to our work.

*Chapter 12*

# Human Rights in International Law

AI's work is based on the principle of international responsibility for the protection of human rights. The rights it is concerned about have been agreed by the member states of the United Nations and other similar bodies. Although AI members are not expected to be experts on international law, it is essential to know the international standards related to AI's work.

## Terms and Definitions

The following are some terms used in international law:

| | |
|---|---|
| Convention & Covenant | — both are formal, legally binding agreements or treaties between sovereign states. The difference in name does not imply any legal difference. |
| Protocol | — a formal, legally binding agreement between sovereign states which is normally a supplement to another treaty or agreement. |
| Declaration | — a general statement of intent or of principle which may not necessarily be legally binding. |
| Ratification | — a decision by a sovereign state to confirm an agreement (as in *ratification* of a treaty). |
| Signature | — indication of the provisional intent of a sovereign state to be bound by the terms of the treaty or agreement. |

**NOTE:** No AI group or member should write direct to any international organization. Write to AI's International Secretariat which maintains links with other such organizations.

## The Universal Declaration of Human Rights

The Universal Declaration of Human Rights is the most commonly accepted statement of "human rights". It was adopted by the United Nations General Assembly on 10 December 1948. The date is commemorated every year by the worldwide observance of Human Rights Day.

The 30 articles of the declaration establish the civil and political, economic, social and cultural rights of all people. The declaration proclaims the right to life, liberty and security of person, to equality before the law without discrimination, to a fair and public trial, to be presumed innocent before proved guilty, to freedom of movement, to freedom of thought, conscience and religion, to freedom of opinion and expression and to freedom of association.

It declares that no one shall be held in slavery, no one shall be subjected to torture or to cruel, inhuman or degrading treatment or punishment and that no one shall be arbitrarily arrested, detained or exiled.

The declaration also establishes that everyone has the right to a nationality, to marry, to own property, to take part in the government of his or her country, to work, to receive equal pay for equal work, to receive just and favourable remuneration, to enjoy rest and leisure and to have an adequate standard of living and education. The declaration further stipulates that everyone has the right to form and join trade unions and the right to seek asylum from persecution.

Many nations have incorporated the provisions of the declaration into their constitutions. It is a statement of principles with an appeal to "every individual and every social organization" to promote and guarantee respect for the freedoms

> *Recognition of the inherent dignity and of the equal and inalienable rights of all members of the human family is the foundation of freedom, justice and peace in the world.*
>
> —*the Universal Declaration of Human Rights*

and rights it defines. United Nations member states were not required to ratify the Universal Declaration of Human Rights (the declaration is not of itself legally binding), although membership in the United Nations is normally considered to be an implicit acceptance of the principles of the declaration. It should be noted that under the Charter of the United Nations, member states are pledged to take joint and separate action to promote universal respect for, and observance of, human rights and fundamental freedoms. This is a legal obligation. The declaration is an authoritative statement of what those human rights and fundamental freedoms are.

## The international human rights covenants

The principles enshrined in the Universal Declaration of Human Rights have been given legal force in two covenants: the International Covenant on Civil and Political Rights and the International Covenant on Economic, Social and Cultural Rights.

The International Covenant on Civil and Political Rights affirms the right to life; prohibits torture or cruel, inhuman or degrading treatment or punishment; prohibits slavery and compulsory labour; prohibits arbitrary arrest and detention; and provides that all those deprived of their liberty shall be treated humanely. It stipulates that anyone sentenced to death has the right to seek pardon or commutation of sentence.

It provides for equality before the courts and tribunals and for safeguards in criminal and civil procedures; prohibits retroactive criminal legislation; establishes the right of everyone to recognition everywhere as a person before the law, and prohibits arbitrary arrest or unlawful interference with privacy, family, home and correspondence. The covenant stipulates the right to freedom of thought, conscience and religion and provides that the law shall guarantee protection from discrimination.

In particular, the covenant defines the acceptable limitations which states may place upon these rights. In time of public emergency, states may "derogate from" (be exempt from) the obligations of the covenant provided this does not involve discrimination solely on the grounds of race, colour, sex, language, religion or social origin and provided certain other conditions are present. Certain rights are considered absolute. No derogation from them may be made even in time of public emergency. These include the right to life, the right not to be subjected to torture or to cruel, inhuman or degrading treatment or punishment, the prohibition of slavery and servitude, the right of everyone to recognition as a person before the law and to freedom of thought, conscience and religion.

The covenant established an 18-member Human Rights Committee which is empowered to consider reports on compliance that parties to the covenant are obliged to provide. But unless a State Party has made a specific declaration recognizing the right of the committee to hear complaints against it by another State Party —so far very few have done so — then the committee has no power to hear such complaints.

The Optional Protocol to the International Covenant on Civil and Political Rights, attached to the covenant, provides a further method of protecting civil and political rights. A state which is party to this protocol recognizes the competence of the Human Rights Committee to consider communications from individuals who claim to be victims of a violation by that state of any rights included in the covenant.

The coming into force in 1976 of the Covenant

on Civil and Political Rights has ushered in a new era in the field of human rights. Over a third of the world's nations are now, for the first time in history, obliged to report publicly to an international body directly responsible for monitoring their performance on what they are doing to ensure for their citizens the rights proclaimed in the Universal Declaration of Human Rights. Their reports are studied, critical questions are asked, and the governments are required to give an account of their human rights records. Often in this process important information and statements have come forth that governments can be held to later on. To question and probe a government has become legitimate. Human rights are no longer an internal affair of states.

# Other international standards

The many other standards set by world bodies such as the United Nations include the following of particular relevance to AI:

● The Standard Minimum Rules for the Treatment of Prisoners. These have been adopted by the Economic and Social Council of the United Nations. They consist of 95 detailed provisions on matters such as accommodation, food, medical services, discipline and punishment, and contacts with the outside world. An important provision, for example, is rule 31 which states that corporal punishment shall be completely prohibited as a punishment for disciplinary offences.

The rules seek "to set out what is generally accepted as being good principle and practice in the treatment of prisoners". They can be invoked in all cases of detention or imprisonment.

● The United Nations Declaration on the Protection of All Persons from Torture and Other Cruel, Inhuman or Degrading Treatment or Punishment. This declaration prohibits torture under all circumstances, obliges all states to conduct a prompt and impartial investigation wherever there are reasonable grounds to believe that torture has been committed; and stipulates that compensation must be given to victims in cases where torture has been proved.

● The Convention relating to the Status of Refugees, its protocol and the United Nations Declaration on Territorial Asylum provide that no one may be forcibly returned to a state where he or she may be persecuted.

● Various codes of ethics for professionals such as doctors and law enforcement officials provide rules on what they should do when faced with the torture and ill-treatment of prisoners.

New standards continue to be drafted by the United Nations and other international organizations. Important examples are the draft Convention Against Torture and the draft Body of Principles for the Protection of all Persons under any Form of Detention or Imprisonment. Rather than giving priority to drafting further human rights standards, however, AI's emphasis is now on seeing that already existing standards are observed.

One of the best compilations of international human rights standards is *Human Rights, A Compilation of International Instruments*, published by the United Nations, sales No. E.78 XIV 2, available from United Nations offices in most countries. A collection of codes of professional ethics may be found in the AI publication *Codes of Professional Ethics*.

# International monitoring bodies

**The United Nations.** Every year thousands of complaints of human rights abuses reach the United Nations, many of whose bodies are directly or indirectly concerned with human rights. Those that have the most to do with AI's concerns are:

1. the Sub-commission on the Prevention of Discrimination and the Protection of Minorities;
2. the Commission on Human Rights;
3. the Economic and Social Council;
4. the General Assembly.

These bodies are in a clear hierarchy, with the sub-commission at the bottom and the General Assembly at the top. Some sub-commission decisions need to be approved by the commission or the council or both; the more important ones need to be approved by the General Assembly as well.

The Sub-commission on the Prevention of Discrimination and the Protection of Minorities consists of 26 independent human rights experts. Although some members are diplomats, many are independent lawyers, judges and professors. As the lowest body in the United Nations' human rights hierarchy, the sub-commissions' main task is to make recommendations to its parent body, the Commission on Human Rights. Although its name does not suggest it, the sub-commission has over the years become increasingly involved with matters of direct concern to AI.

The Commission on Human Rights is the main United Nations body responsible for human rights questions. It consists of 43 members appointed by governments regularly selected by the Economic and Social Council. It has the authority to examine "particular situations which appear to reveal a consistent pattern of gross and reliably attested violations of human rights". Communications about human rights violations may be submitted by non-governmental organizations. These must show that all possible remedies on the national level have been sought or would be ineffective. A communication, if accepted, goes first to a Working Group and then to the Sub-commission on the Prevention of Discrimination and the Protection of Minorities. The matter is then referred to the commission itself which may decide to make further investigations and submit a report to the Economic and Social Council.

# The Human Rights Committee

The International Covenant on Civil and Political Rights provides for an 18-member Human Rights Committee. The members serve in their own personal capacities and, according to the covenant, should be of "high moral character and recognized competence in the field of human rights".

This committee should not be confused with the United Nations Commission on Human Rights. The committee is responsible to the States Parties to the covenant and is independent of the United Nations apart from having to send an annual report to the General Assembly. Its

In the chamber of the United Nations General Assembly, Amnesty International receives the 1978 United Nations Human Rights Prize.

stated intention is to establish a dialogue with the States Parties in order to achieve respect for the rights set forth in the covenant. By making recommendations and giving advice it tries to help States Parties overcome any obstacles to ensure to their citizens the rights set forth in the covenant. It is not empowered to recommend sanctions against a State Party which violates the covenant.

# UNESCO

Like other intergovernmental agencies UNESCO (the United Nations Educational, Scientific and Cultural Organization) has adopted a number of conventions and recommendations on human rights. In 1978 the Executive Board of UNESCO adopted procedures for dealing with reports of human rights violations relevant to UNESCO provided such reports came from victims or people with reliable information about the violations. Several hundred such communications are received on average each year. UNESCO also aims to promote human rights education, both in schools and in the community as a whole.

# International Labour Organisation (ILO)

The ILO has adopted many standards, among them several dealing with issues of concern to AI such as forced labour (involving political prisoners) and freedom of association. It has a variety of procedures to monitor abuses of these standards. Information on such questions must be submitted to the ILO through one of its three constituencies: trade unions, employers' organizations or governments.

# Regional human rights standards

## Africa

The Heads of States of the Organization of African Unity (OAU) decided in July 1979 to draw up a charter of "human and peoples' rights" and create machinery for monitoring compliance with it. This was completed in 1981. The charter will come into force when ratified by a majority of OAU members and will establish the African Commission on Human and Peoples'

Rights. Already, AI has on occasion submitted information on human rights questions to the Chairman of the OAU.

## Americas

The Organization of American States (OAS) has adopted several important human rights instruments: the Bogota Charter which established the structure of the Organization, the American Declaration of the Rights and Duties of Man which proclaims a number of individual rights and obligations and the Inter-American Charter of Social Guarantees which sets forth labour and social rights.

The American Convention on Human Rights, the legally binding document for the protection of human rights in the Americas, was adopted in 1969 and entered into force in 1978 after ratification by the necessary minimum 11 member states of the OAS.

The Inter-American Commission on Human Rights comprises seven members who are individuals from countries belonging to the OAS, acting in their personal capacities. It has a procedure for the examination of communications submitted to it but the findings of the commission are not binding upon any government. Communications may be submitted by individuals and non-governmental organizations. The commission examines evidence submitted to it and sends a draft report to the government concerned. If the government does not respond or take sufficient account of the recommendations, the commission may prepare a study of human rights in that country and, if violations are proved, may make recommendations to both the state concerned and the General Assembly of the OAS. It may also make on-site inspections with the consent of the government in question.

The Inter-American Court of Human Rights is the other body established by the American Convention on Human Rights to protect human rights but it has jurisdiction only in relation to states which have made the declaration recognizing the jurisdiction of the court as determined by Article 62 of the American Convention on Human Rights. Few states have accepted the jurisdiction of the court which has therefore been limited to an advisory role within the meaning of Article 64 of the American Convention on Human Rights.

## Asia

The idea of a regional human rights mechanism for Asia has been proposed several times and discussed at United Nations level, but as yet no inter-governmental body has been created. Non-governmental groups in the region have brought together human rights lawyers and other activists from time to time and have discussed the value of encouraging official regional mechanisms. In November 1981 an All-Asia Bar Association was formed at a meeting of 72 lawyers from 13 Asian countries at Kochi in Japan. Among the immediate principal activities of the association were to be the protection of lawyers in the performance of their professional duties, the monitoring of the human rights situation in each country and the promotion of human rights.

## Europe

The Council of Europe has adopted several human rights instruments, among them the European Convention on Human Rights.

The rights set forth in this convention are based partly on the Universal Declaration of Human Rights. The convention includes elaborate implementation procedures. Under its terms a Commission and Court of Human Rights have been set up which, together with the Committee of Ministers of the Council of Europe, a political body, are responsible for the implementation of the convention.

The Council of Europe's Parliamentary Assembly recommended in 1980 that the convention be amended so that it would no longer allow for the death penalty in time of peace. The assembly has also recommended that the right of conscientious objection to military service be included in the convention. Both proposals require a decision by the Committee of Ministers before they can be put into effect.

The European Commission on Human Rights consists of one member for each state which is party to the European Convention on Human Rights, acting in their personal capacities. Petitions may be submitted by individuals, non-governmental organizations or groups of individuals who claim to be victims of violations of the rights guaranteed by the convention where parties have accepted the right of individual petition. Governments have the automatic right to make complaints about alleged violations of human rights by another government. A situation will be brought before either the European Court of Human Rights or the Committee of Ministers following investigation by the commission. The Committee of Ministers can prescribe certain measures to be taken by the state concerned. The decisions of the committee and the court are binding.

## The Middle East

Official machinery for the protection of human rights, similar to that in Europe and the Americas, does not yet exist in the Middle East, but there have been efforts in this direction. In May 1979 the Union of Arab Jurists agreed to a Draft Arab Covenant on Human Rights. Although it was designed merely to promote wider discussion of the issue and has no legal status, it is a significant indication of the needs felt by jurists in the Arab world. The draft covenant was adopted at a symposium on "Human Rights and Fundamental Freedoms in the Arab Homeland" which also recommended the creation of a permanent non-governmental Arab Committee to protect human rights and fundamental freedoms in the Arab world. The proposed committee would include representatives of popular and professional institutions as well as prominent figures known for their efforts on behalf of human rights and freedoms.

A series of detailed circulars describing AI's work with international organizations was issued in 1979 and 1980. These are available from all sections under the general AI Index category: IOR 03.

# Chapter 13

# Working Rules

The Working Rules were first adopted by the International Council in 1976. They have now been revised in accordance with subsequent decisions of the Council and the International Executive Committee.

The rules do not and cannot cover all questions that arise in AI's activities. They give the framework within which all members are expected to work. The principle underlying the rules is that all parts of the Amnesty International movement should follow consistent policies and procedures since statements or activities by any member, group or section may be taken as representing the organization as a whole.

## Publicity and Publications

**1.** The term "publications" refers to news releases, newsletters, reports, films, sound or video tapes, leaflets and posters intended for public use. All publications must be in accordance with AI's mandate and respect the organization's standards of accuracy and impartiality.

**2.** Amnesty International Publications (AIPs) are issued by the International Secretariat under the authority of the International Executive Committee.

**3.** AI sections are responsible for all AI publications, other than AIPs, issued in their country or territory. This applies to their translations of AIPs and external documents issued by the International Secretariat as well as to publications drafted by AI groups in the section. All publications must clearly indicate the authority under which they are issued (for example, "published by the Mexican Section of Amnesty International").

**4.** Any publication prepared by an AI section that includes information other than that based on recent external AI information must be submitted for comment and approval to the International Secretariat. Sections are advised to consult the secretariat before issuing any major publication on a country or issue, even if it is based on external AI information to ensure proper coordination of international efforts.

**5.** AI sections are required to draw up guidelines for their membership on relations with the news media in their country or territory. They are to appoint a press officer responsible for coordination of all such relations and for liaison with the Press Office of the International Secretariat.

**6.** Any news release, information material or statement to be issued to the news media by an AI section, other than that based on recent external AI information, must be submitted for comment and approval to the International Secretariat.

**7.** An AI section wishing to mention or list names of prisoners in a publication or statement is required to use only names of prisoners whose cases have been allocated to groups in that section or mentioned in recent external AI information.

**8.** Groups must strictly observe the instructions in all prisoner dossiers about publicity on particular cases.

**9.** AI sections are responsible for the preparation and use of audio-visual materials in their country or territory. Care must be taken to ensure that they reflect AI's mandate and conform to its standards of accuracy and impartiality. In particular, the abuse of national symbols should be avoided.

**10.** The International Executive Committee has the authority to review and if necessary prohibit any document or statement by an AI section if there is reason to believe that it would create undesirable international repercussions. The International Executive Committee also has the right to disclaim publicly any publication not issued in accordance with the procedures and guidelines established by the International Council.

# Statements on members' countries

**11.** AI sections are not empowered to make statements or to issue publications about the human rights situation in their own countries or territories, apart from matters to do with ratification of treaties and changes in legislation on the death penalty. Any exceptions to this rule must be decided by the International Executive Committee in consultation with the section concerned.

**12.** In response to inquiries about human rights violations in its own country or territory an AI section is required to explain that responsibility for AI policy on such matters lies with the International Executive Committee. The section may refer such inquiries to the International Secretariat or provide without further elaboration any available AI external information and state that AI has taken action on behalf of individual prisoners if this is the case.

**13.** AI sections may be provided with copies of Amnesty International publications and external documents on their own countries or territories, if they so request, and may distribute such documents.

# External relations

**14.** AI sections are required to appoint people responsible for contacts with their own government, visits to embassies and contacts with other organizations, and to draw up guidelines and procedures for such contacts.

**15.** It is not the responsibility of an AI section to make representations to its own government about human rights violations in its own country or territory. Such representations are the responsibility of the International Executive Committee and of other sections acting on information provided by the International Secretariat. An AI section may make representations to its own government about violations of human rights in its own country or territory only if authorized to do so by the International Executive Committee. In making any such authorized representation the section should always stress that its action reflects the concern of the international movement.

**16.** AI members should not write to third party governments (governments in countries other than their own or the target country) or representatives of third party governments unless they are specifically requested or authorized to do so by the International Secretariat.

**17.** Relations with international non-governmental organizations and intergovernmental organizations are the responsibility of the International Secretariat acting under the authority of the International Executive Committee. AI sections, groups and members should not write to headquarters or officials of intergovernmental bodies (such as the United Nations) or to international non-governmental organizations unless specifically requested to do so by the International Secretariat. Sections wishing to approach non-governmental organizations in other countries must consult the AI section of that country or the International Secretariat if there is no section.

**18.** AI may provide and exchange external information with other organizations and may send representatives to attend their meetings and speak on matters within AI's mandate. However, no public actions such as news conferences, demonstrations or public meetings may be organized or sponsored jointly by AI and any other organization without the approval of the relevant AI section governing body. Nor may any group or member sign any other organization's appeals or resolutions in the name of AI without section approval. The International Secretariat advises against any such joint activities with other organizations, particularly on country-related matters. It should be emphasized to other organizations that AI does not undertake joint activities with other bodies in order to protect its independence and impartiality. This policy does not reflect either approval or disapproval of the aims or judgments of other organizations.

# Case work and campaigns

**19.** AI sections are expected to inform the International Secretariat of their plans for participation in campaigns and actions announced in the Action Calendar issued by the International Secretariat. Any plans for other major section campaigns should be discussed with the International Secretariat to ensure proper international coordination.

**20.** Any action initiated by one section (including international appeals on behalf of one prisoner) which would involve members and groups in other sections must not be undertaken without prior consultation with the International Secretariat. This includes actions by coordination and professional groups.

**21.** AI sections, groups and members are required to send any new prisoner-related information they collect to the International Secretariat. Sections, groups or members who wish to do research work are required to consult the International Secretariat.

**22.** AI groups are required to follow carefully the instructions and recommended actions provided in the *Amnesty International Handbook*, the "general instructions" and "recommended actions" included in each prisoner dossier and to observe carefully the difference between adoption and investigation cases as explained in "Status of Case" documents in each dossier. The decision to adopt or investigate any case rests with the International Secretariat. No unusual action should be undertaken without prior consultation with the relevant coordination group, section or International Secretariat.

**23.** If a case has been closed by the International Secretariat, group activities on the prisoner's behalf must cease. Private initiatives may be undertaken on the prisoner's behalf, but all correspondence must be signed by someone other than the group members who have previously been writing about the case to the authorities.

**24.** Exiles, refugees and other foreign nationals who are members or supporters of AI are not permitted to send letters to government authorities in their own country. Where such nationals are members of local groups, they should not be involved in case work on their own country but should work on behalf of other prisoners.

# Missions/AI travel

**25.** The term "mission" refers to visits to countries by an individual or team to conduct business on behalf of Amnesty International relating to its concerns, or to discuss membership questions on behalf of the International Executive Committee. All AI missions must be approved and funded by the International Executive Committee. The briefing of AI missions is the responsibility of the International Secretariat.

**26.** It is not the responsibility of an AI section to plan, brief or collaborate with an AI mission sent to its country or territory.

**27.** An AI section shall be notified in advance of a mission to its country or territory, subject to considerations of security and confidentiality. If the section has been notified of the mission, it may respond to inquiries only by confirming the arrival of the mission and stating its terms of reference.

**28.** No visit to a country by any AI member shall be considered an AI mission unless it has been approved as such by the International Executive Committee.

**29.** Coordination group members are required to consult the International Secretariat before travelling to the countries with which their group is concerned. This procedure applies even when they are travelling in their private capacity.

**30.** AI members travelling in their private capacity are not authorized to undertake AI business such as research or work related to relief or individual prisoner cases (including those allocated to their group) without first consulting and receiving the approval of the International Secretariat. This procedure does not apply to visits involving normal consultation and discussion within the movement on organizational matters.

**31.** AI groups wishing to send members to countries to visit prisoners or prisoners' families are required to consult and obtain the approval of the International Secretariat in advance and if possible to obtain the consent of the family before making such a visit. Any other activities (such as distribution of relief, visits to lawyers or contacts) in the course of such a visit are also subject to the approval of the International Secretariat. Such visits are not AI missions and members are not empowered to speak or act in the name of AI.

**32.** AI members travelling in their private capacity or on behalf of other organizations should make every effort to avoid the impression that they represent AI or are travelling on AI business. If asked, they must stress that they have no authority to make any statement related to AI or its concerns.

**33.** AI members travelling in their private capacity to countries in which there are major AI concerns are advised to inform their section beforehand.

# International cooperation

**34.** All constituent bodies of AI are expected to cooperate with other parts of the movement in working for the aims of AI.

**35.** Local groups must observe the guidelines for double and triple adoptions. Coordination groups must cooperate closely with the relevant coordination groups in other sections. Professional groups must cooperate closely with related professional groups and committees in other sections.

**36.** AI sections are required to inform the International Secretariat of the names and responsibilities of the elected officers of the section, staff members and other individuals or groups appointed to undertake functions on behalf of the section board. They are also required to inform the secretariat of the changes of address of their section office, groups and other bodies within the section.

**37.** AI sections are required to submit an annual report on their activities to the International Executive Committee.

**38.** AI groups are required to submit reports on their prisoner-related activities to the International Secretariat and their sections every six months. New information obtained about any case should be reported immediately to the International Secretariat.

**39.** Coordination groups and professional groups are required to submit reports on their activities to the International Secretariat and their sections twice a year.

**40.** No AI section, group or member shall ask a section, group or member in another country or territory for information about human rights questions or prisoner cases there.

**41.** Correspondence from AI members to the International Executive Committee must be channelled through their section. Correspondence to the International Executive Committee or its individual members should be sent to the Secretary General's Office at the International Secretariat.

**42.** AI sections may make complaints to the International Executive Committee and, if they are not satisfied with the response, to the International Council. In the event of disagreement between a coordination or other group and any part of the International Secretariat, the relevant AI section may bring the matter to the attention of the Secretary General. If the disagreement involves a question of AI policy and is not resolved the matter shall be referred to the International Executive Committee and, if necessary, to the International Council. Every effort shall be made to resolve any dispute without publicity.

# Finance, fund-raising and relief

**43.** AI sections are required to appoint a treasurer and to submit standardized financial reports each year to the international Treasurer.

**44.** AI sections are required to adhere to the Guidelines for the Acceptance of Financial Contributions and Fund-raising to Amnesty International.

**45.** No fund-raising project shall be carried out by a constituent body of AI in another country where there is an AI section without the consent of that section.

**46.** AI sections must appoint a relief officer to ensure the section's adherence to AI's relief policy and procedures and advise groups and members on their relief activities. Relief payments to individual prisoners, released prisoners or prisoners' families must be made in accordance with the recommendations of the International Secretariat and be reported to the secretariat every six months.

**47.** An AI section or coordination group may operate a relief program on behalf of the International Secretariat only with the agreement of the Relief Committee and the section concerned.

# Membership, internal structures and information handling

**48.** AI sections and groups are required to observe the guidelines for sections and groups adopted by the International Council.

**49.** Recognition of an AI section is the responsibility of the International Executive Committee. The section's statute must be in accordance with the AI Statute. Any changes in a section's statute concerning aims, methods and objects must be approved by the International Executive Committee before they come into force.

**50.** AI section governing bodies are responsible for the proper functioning of the AI membership in their country or territory. The governing body reviews the activities of the members and groups, ensures their proper functioning and has the power to close groups or terminate membership or recommend such action to the International Secretariat when the work of such groups or individuals is prejudicial to AI.

**51.** AI section governing bodies are responsible for approving groups before asking the International Secretariat to register them.

**52.** Members of the International Executive Committee and of the International Secretariat and other AI bodies shall, in the exercise of their AI functions, refrain from any action incompatible with their functions. In particular they shall not seek or accept instructions from any national or international entity, other than AI bodies.

**53.** Members of AI section governing bodies and senior staff members are required to observe the guidelines, "Public Role of Members of AI Section Governing Bodies and Senior Staff Members", recommended by the International Council.

**54.** Coordination groups are required to observe the rule that members of the group should not be nationals of the country involved, exiles from that country or individuals with political affiliations or interests which would reduce their political objectivity.

**55.** Coordination groups are required to consult the International Secretariat before establishing information contacts outside their own country.

**56.** AI sections, groups and members are required to observe strictly the guidelines on responsible handling of information. All internal documents issued by the sections and coordination groups should be clearly marked as internal.

**57.** AI sections are required to appoint a member responsible for security who should maintain contact as necessary with the International Secretariat and recommend measures to protect the section's offices, information and activities.

**58.** Consistent failure on the part of AI sections, groups and members to observe security instructions, including those listed in the *Amnesty International Handbook* and all prisoner dossiers, may be drawn to the attention of the International Executive Committee and may result in restricted access to sensitive materials.

# Chapter 14

# Commonly Asked Questions

**1. Where does Amnesty International get its money from?**

Amnesty International relies on donations from its members and the public. It must continue to be — and be seen to be — financially independent. By far the greatest part of the movement's funds come from small individual donations, membership fees, and local fund-raising drives. These help to build a broad popular movement, backed up by financial support from the public throughout the world.

**2. What about money from governments?**

AI does not seek or receive government money for its budget. It will accept contributions for humanitarian relief to prisoners, but only if AI administers the funds itself. Under no circumstances will it accept donations from any source earmarked for work on a specific country or case.

**3. How does Amnesty International get its information?**

AI uses a wide variety of sources, both public and private. The International Secretariat subscribes to hundreds of newspapers and journals and gets transcriptions of radio broadcasts, government bulletins, reports from legal experts, letters from prisoners and their families. It also sends fact-finding missions to assess situations on the spot, interview prisoners and meet government officials.

**4. How does Amnesty International make sure it has the facts right?**

All information that reaches the International Secretariat is carefully sifted by the research staff. Details are cross-checked and care is taken to avoid presenting any unconfirmed allegation as a fact. Before any statement is issued the text is vetted at several different levels of the secretariat to make sure it is accurate and comes within AI's mandate.

**5. Isn't Amnesty International a political organization?**

AI is impartial. It does not support or oppose any government or political system. It believes human rights must be respected universally. It takes up cases whenever it considers there are reliable grounds for concern, regardless of the ideology of the government or the beliefs of the victims.

**6. Isn't Amnesty International interfering in the internal affairs of states?**

Human rights transcend national boundaries. This principle has been recognized by the world's main intergovernmental organizations. The very fact that the United Nations has a permanent Commission on Human Rights which deals with human rights violations around the world is proof that the human rights practices of individual governments are a legitimate concern for scrutiny by the international community. AI works on that principle and seeks observance of the human rights standards that governments themselves have adopted internationally.

**7. Why does Amnesty International take up cases of people who have broken their country's laws?**

National laws themselves often violate international human rights standards. In many countries emergency legislation drastically curtails the rights of all citizens and provides for lengthy detention without charge or trial. In examining each situation, AI uses a single, universal standard — internationally recognized human rights. If a state is violating those rights, AI comes to the defence of the victims.

**8. What is AI's position on abuses committed by opposition groups?**

AI holds as a matter of principle that the torture and execution of prisoners by anyone, including opposition groups, can never be accepted. Governments have the responsibility of dealing with such abuses, acting in conformity with international standards for the protection of human rights.

**9. Why does Amnesty International oppose torture and the death penalty in *all* cases?**
Both are cruel, inhuman and degrading. The United Nations has declared an absolute ban on torture, recognizing that there are no circumstances under which it can be justified. It has also recognized the desirability of abolishing the death penalty, which is an unjust and irrevocable punishment. AI's opposition to the cruel treatment of prisoners does not mean that it condones any violent crimes of which they may be suspected or convicted. At the same time, it insists that there are no circumstances under which the state is justified in torturing or executing its own citizens.

**10. What countries does Amnesty International regard as the worst violators of human rights?**
AI does not grade governments according to their human rights records or establish a "blacklist". Not only does repression in various countries prevent the free flow of information about human rights abuses, but the techniques of repression and their impact vary widely. Instead of attempting comparisons AI concentrates on trying to end the specific violations of human rights in each case.

**11. Aren't human rights a luxury, especially in less developed countries?**
There can be no double standard on human rights. They apply to everyone everywhere. Nor do economic, social and cultural rights conflict with civil and political rights; both are essential in any society at all stages of development.

**12. What does Amnesty International do for political prisoners who have used or advocated violence?**
AI takes no position on the question of violence. It opposes the torture and execution of all prisoners and advocates fair and prompt trials for all political prisoners, regardless of whether they are accused of using or advocating violence. However, AI seeks the immediate and unconditional *release* only of individuals imprisoned for the *non-violent* exercise of their human rights as their very detention violates the Universal Declaration of Human Rights.

**13. Does AI get results?**
AI has helped increase public awareness throughout the world about political imprisonment, torture and the death penalty. This awareness has prompted the news media to pay much more attention to human rights violations. AI has also helped promote improved international standards for the protection of human rights. Bodies like the United Nations have taken important steps, such as declaring a universal ban on torture. Perhaps most significant is the fact that many prisoners, their families and lawyers have thanked AI for its efforts on their behalf. Although AI does not claim credit for the release of prisoners, many former prisoners have said that it was international pressure that secured their freedom or saved their lives.

**14. What do Amnesty International members do about human rights in their own country?**
As an individual citizen or as a member of a civil liberties group, anyone is free to become involved in domestic cases or causes. However, when working for AI they must respect the principle of *international* protection of human rights. AI members and groups do not work on cases in their own countries or make statements about them. Under AI's rules, however, they may work for the abolition of the death penalty in their own country, press their own government to ratify international human rights treaties, try to ensure that refugees are not sent back to countries where they might face torture or execution or become prisoners of conscience, and play a part in local human rights education programs.

**15. Is it true that Amnesty International has links with intelligence agencies?**
No. AI is independent of all governments and government agencies. It acts openly and does not conduct espionage. No evidence has ever been produced to substantiate claims —made by governments of the left and right — that AI is linked in any way to national intelligence services.

**16. How do Amnesty International members participate in policy-making?**
AI is a participatory movement. Through the groups and sections members decide on the policy of the movement they finance. All sections have their own internal structures for involving their members and send representatives to the International Council meeting where delegates from all over the world determine the movement's program.

After three years in one of Haiti's most dreaded prisons, Marc Romulus was reunited with his son, Patrice. The 34-year-old teacher had been arrested on suspicion of opposing the government. An Amnesty International group in the Federal Republic of Germany was put to work on the case. The government said he was one of a number of "unknown persons" but the Amnesty International campaign continued. It took two years for the government to admit he was in detention, although he was then described as an "unrepentant terrorist". Amnesty International continued to work on Marc Romulus' behalf. In September 1977 he was included in an amnesty for political prisoners. The man who the government at one stage said did not exist was at last reunited with his family.

# Index

Acceptance of funds, see Fund-raising
Addresses 59
Administration Department 30
Adoption 8, 52
  double and triple 53
Advisory Group on Information Handling and
  Technology 27
Aftercare 55
Amnesties 9
Annual report 20, 36, 39
Appeals 17, 44, 45
Approaches to companies 22
Approaches to other organizations 43, 57, 90

Benenson, Peter 3
Borderline Committee 27

Campaign and Membership Department 29, 51
Campaign for the Abolition of Torture 15
  see also Torture
Campaign for the Prisoners of the Month 18, 20, 23
Campaigns 15, 90
Case sheet 53
Case work 14, 15, 50-58, 77, 89
Codes of Ethics 16, 85
Commercial relations 22
Committees, international 27-28
Commonly Asked Questions 94
Companies, approaches to 22
Conferences, AI international 12, 15, 16, 17
Conscientious Objection 9, 72-73
Contacts, AI 57
Cooperation with other organizations 43, 57, 90
Coordination 42, 51
Coordination groups 25, 51
Coordinators, country 25
  campaigns 19
  Regional Action Networks 19
  target sector 21
  Urgent Actions 17
Correspondence with
  AI contacts 57
  government authorities 55, 56
  the International Secretariat 51
  prisoner and family 58
  see also Letters
Council, see International Council
Country campaigns 19
Covenants, international human rights: see
  International

Death penalty 10, 11, 12, 16, 17, 73-74, 78, 95
Decision making in AI 27
Declaration of Stockholm 17, 73-74
Declaration on the Protection of All Persons from
  Torture and Other Cruel, Inhuman or Degrading
  Treatment or Punishment 85
Delegations 45, 56
Demonstrations 46
"Disappearances" 12, 53
Documentation Centre 29
Double adoption 53

Education, human rights 22, 49
Educational institutions 48
Embassies 45, 56
Emigration, see Refugees
Espionage 9
European Commission on Human Rights 88
European Communities 21
Europe, Council of 21, 88
Evaluation of Techniques, committee for
  systematic 27
Executions 11
  see also Death Penalty
Executive Assistants 29, 51
Exile organizations 43
Extrajudicial executions 11, 12

Fair trial 9, 10, 52
Families 58
Films 46
Finances 31, 34, 67, 92
Financial Control Committee 27, 34
Fund-raising 31-33, 92, 94
  guidelines 34, 80-82

Governments, approaches to 55, 56
  national, representations to 20, 78, 90
Group cases 53
Groups
  AI local 24, 50-58
  coordination 25
  guidelines 74-77
  professional 21, 25-26
Guidelines
  for Acceptance of Financial Contributions 80-82
  for Sections and Groups 74-77
  on Conscientious Objection 72
  on AI sections' activities concerning human
    rights violations in their own countries 77-80

Human Rights Committee 84, 86
Human Rights Education 22, 49

Impartiality 9, 14, 34, 36, 40, 68
    Impartiality and the Defence of Human Rights
    68-70
Information, see Research
InfoTech 27
Inter-American Commission on Human Rights 87
International Executive Committee (IEC) 26, 66
International Committee of the Red Cross 12
International committees 26-27
International Council (ICM) 7, 25, 65-66
International Covenant on Civil and Political
    Rights 84, 86
International Covenant on Economic, Social and
    Cultural Rights 84
International Labour Organisation (ILO) 87
International Organizations, relations with 21, 43,
    90
International Secretariat (IS) 14, 28, 29, 51, 67
Investigation 8, 9, 10, 52, 53

Killings, political by governments 11-12

Language 51, 59
Lawyers groups 21
Legal Aid 10
Legal Office 29
Letters 18, 44, 59-62
Lobbying 45, 49
Local groups, see Groups

Mandate 7, 15, 40, 64
Media, news 35-38
    see also Press relations and Publicity
Medical Advisory Board 16, 27
Medical groups 16, 21
Members 23, 24, 65
Military, security and police transfers 22
Missions 19, 20, 78, 91

Newsletter 16, 18, 20, 36, 39
News media 35-38
    see also Press relations and Publicity
News releases 37, 38
Nobel Peace Prize 6
Non-governmental organizations, see
    International Organizations and Target Sector
    Work

Organization of African Unity (OAU) 13, 87
Organization of American States (OAS) 21, 87
Organizations, international 21, 43, 90

PAI (Publicaciones Amnistía Internacional) 30
Performances 47

Petitions 18, 44
Political killings by governments 11, 12
Political parties 49
Political prisoners 9
Political trials 9, 10
Press and Publications Department 30
Press Officers 36-38
Press relations 35-38, 56
Pressure 43
Prison conditions 12, 13, 80
Prisoner dossier 52, 53
Prisoners of Conscience 7, 8, 9, 52
Prisoners of Conscience Week 18
Prisoners of the Month Campaign 18
Public actions 18, 46
Publications 20, 35, 39, 79, 89
Publicity 18, 20, 35-38, 56, 79, 89

Questions, commonly asked 94

Ratification of treaties 78
Refugees 13, 79, 85
Regional Action Networks 19
Regional human rights standards 87
Relations with other organizations 43, 57, 90
Relief 20, 58, 80, 92
Religious groups 22, 48
Reporting 50
Representations to national governments 20, 78, 90
Research 14
Research Department 8, 14, 29, 51
Researchers 8, 29
Responsibilities of an AI Group 50-58
Responsible handling of information 42, 50

Sample letters 60-62
SAPS (South Asia Publications Service) 30
Schools 22
Secretariat, see International Secretariat
Secretary General 28
Sections 25-26
Security 42, 50, 93
Special actions 19
Standard Minimum Rules for the Treatment of
    Prisoners 12, 13, 85
Statute 7, 36, 63-67
Stockholm Declaration 17, 73-74
Subscribers 23-24
Symbolic actions 47
SYSTEC (Committee for Systematic Evaluation of
    Techniques) 27

Target Sector Work 21, 22, 47-49
Teachers groups 22
Telegrams 59, 62
Torture 10, 17, 95
    Campaign for the Abolition of 10, 15-16
Trade Unions 21, 47-48

Travel, see Missions
Treasurer 26, 34, 66
Trials, political 9, 10
Triple adoption 53


Urgent Actions 16, 17-18, 23
Unité francophone 30
United Nations 16, 21, 83, 84, 85
    UNESCO 21, 87
    UN Commission on Human Rights 21, 86
    UN Congress on the Prevention of Crime and the
        Treatment of Offenders 12, 17
    UN High Commissioner for Refugees 13

UN Sub-Commission on the Prevention of
    Discrimination and the Protection of
    Minorities 86
Universal Declaration of Human Rights 83


Violence 9, 70
    AI and the Use of Violence 70-72
Visits 38, 91
    see also Delegations and Missions


Weekly Update Service 36
Working Rules 89-93